Covering Campaigns

Covering Campaigns

JOURNALISM IN
CONGRESSIONAL ELECTIONS

*

Peter Clarke and Susan H. Evans

Stanford University Press, Stanford, California

1983

Stanford University Press, Stanford, California

© 1983 by the Board of Trustees of the
Leland Stanford Junior University

Printed in the United States of America
ISBN 0-8047-1159-3   LC 82-60738

Some of the findings in Chapters Two, Four, and Six have appeared, in different form, in earlier publications: "All in a Day's Work: Reporters Covering
Congressional Campaigns," *Journal of Communication*, 30 (1980); "By Pen
or by Pocketbook? Voter Understanding of Congressional Contenders," in
Individuals in Mass Media Organizations: Creativity and Constraint, ed.
James S. Ettema and D. Charles Whitney (SAGE: Beverly Hills, Calif., 1982);
and "Press Coverage and Competition for House Seats," paper presented to
the annual meeting of the American Political Science Association,
New York City, 1981.

To CHRIS, with his wizardry
at computer accounts,
and to MADIE and JACK, for
the spark to keep going

Acknowledgments

DIFFERENT VIEWS about media and politics have contributed to our inquiry and the interpretation of the results. Warren Miller, former Director of the University of Michigan's Center for Political Studies, provided unending support and a lively reading of an early draft of this manuscript. Fred Currier of Market Opinion Research suggested alternative explanations where results seemed especially puzzling. James Naughton of the *Philadelphia Inquirer* and Ben Bagdikian, a veteran national journalist now at the University of California, Berkeley, were generous with their time and comments.

Peter B. Clark gave us an unusual blend of reactions, reflecting his years as publisher of the *Detroit News* and his academic training as a political scientist. Celinda Lake, at the University of Michigan, wrote thoughtful notations on every page we gave her. John Kingdon, David Paletz, Steve Chaffee, Bill Porter, Gary Jacobson, and Al Cover generously shared reactions drawn from their own studies of politics and communication.

For three years of data collection, analysis, and writing, the Howard R. Marsh Center for the Study of Journalistic Performance provided continuous support. We are grateful to this arm of the University of Michigan's Department of Communication.

Judy Timberg's deft and unflagging editorial skills alerted us to awkward and misleading passages. Finally, we thank the hundreds of reporters, editors, and political insiders who responded to our interviews or joined us for extended conversations about our results.

P.C.

S.H.E.

Contents

Tables and Figures

Covering Campaigns

I

Journalism and Politics Reconsidered

THE JOURNALIST strides across comic pages, stage, and literature, a powerful and romantic figure. This mythical character banishes evil, exalts good government, and rescues the needy from the perils of complex society. It is the storyteller who fuels popular images of the press.

The most famous reporter of all time is Clark Kent. This mild-mannered, bespectacled young man and his colleagues—Lois Lane, cub Jimmy Olsen, and gruff editor Perry White—have become familiar through comics, television, and movies. As Clark Kent figured it, there was no more desirable profession to enter than journalism: "If I get news dispatches promptly, I'll be in a better position to help people. I've got to get this job" (*Superman* 1971).

In 1928, Broadway saw corrupt Chicago politicians meet their match in the hard-nosed journalistic antics of *The Front Page*. Reporter Hildy Johnson and editor Walter Burns's zest for a good lead captures the guile, exuberance, and arrogance that was so much a part of the news business (Hecht & Mac-Arthur 1928: 120):

WALTER: What's your lead?
HILDY: (*with authorly pride*) While hundreds of Sheriff Hartman's paid gunmen stalked through Chicago shooting innocent bystanders, spreading their reign of terror, Earl Williams was lurking less than twenty yards from the Sheriff's office where . . .
WALTER: That's *lousy!* Aren't you going to mention *The Examiner?* Don't we take *any* credit?

HILDY: I'm putting that in the second paragraph . . .
WALTER: Who the hell's going to read the second paragraph? Ten
   years I've been telling you how to write a newspaper story— My
   God, have I got to do everything? Get the story? Write the story?

Evelyn Waugh's firsthand experience formed the basis for
a comic newspaper adventure in which neither war correspondents nor Fleet Street escaped unscathed. The *Megalo-
politan's* unflinching commitment to comprehensive coverage sets a tough standard (Waugh 1937: 14):

"Who will you be sending to Ishmaelia?" asked Mrs. Stitch.
"I am in consultation with my editors on the subject. We think
that it is a very promising little war. A microcosm as you might say
of world drama. We propose to give it fullest publicity. The work-
ings of a great newspaper," said Lord Copper, feeling at last thoroughly Rotarian, "are of a complexity which the public seldom ap-
preciates. The citizen little realizes the vast machinery put into
motion for him in exchange for his morning penny. We shall have
our naval, military and air experts, our squad of photographers, our
colour reporters, covering the war from every angle and on every
front."
"Yes," said Mrs. Stitch, "yes, yes. I suppose you will . . . If I were
you I should send someone like Boot. I don't suppose you could
persuade *him* to go, but someone like him."
"It has been my experience, dear Mrs. Stitch, that the *Megalopol-
itan* can command the talent of the world. Only last week the Poet
Laureate wrote us an ode to the seasonal fluctuation of our net sales.
We splashed it on the middle page. He admitted it was the most po-
etic and highly paid work he had ever done."

We can glean an important lesson from folk and literary
heroes in journalism. Without exception they are adventur-
ers who battle against wrongdoing, champion the meek, or
conquer foreign assignments as matters of individual combat. They do not pry into the political system or rail against
social injustices on the broad scale that leads to legislation,
judicial action, or electoral overthrow.

This popular portrait of journalists draws realistic as well
as imaginary lines. The following study reveals how journalistic habits favor the political status quo, seldom reporting
challenges to existing institutional arrangements. Politics is
an uncomfortable place for courageous and unfettered reporting, as a recent landmark case suggests. Insiders at the
Washington Post are fond of recalling how the paper's man-

aging editor was awakened by a call telling him of the Watergate break-in at the Democratic party headquarters. He sleepily decided that it was a crime story, not a piece of political intrigue. Happily, reporters from the metropolitan desk stayed with the investigation to its bitter and highly political conclusion several years later. Those journalists' initial insensitivity to the currents of power politics steadied their course, where others might have shrunk from implications of the unfolding story.

But we need not depend on Watergate as a reason to examine work ways of the press and their political implications. Democratic self-government assumes access to information, without which citizens are limited in their ability to perform essential roles. The social responsibility theory asserts that the press, enjoying a privileged position under the Constitution, is charged with serving the political system by "providing information, discussion, and debate on public affairs, and enlightening the public" (Peterson 1956: 74).

No more demanding test of this charge can be found than the electoral process. Individual political careers and party fortunes respond to the way in which voters' choices are shaped by media portrayals and by the selective filters through which information passes. The story we uncover in the following pages looks at one corner of the media; it describes and helps to explain political reporting and editorializing by newspapers in the heat of congressional elections.*

This study represents an important shift in a long-standing media-and-politics research tradition. Instead of media-reliance patterns among voters, we look at work patterns among a national sample of media professionals. Instead of presidential elections, our eye focuses on congressional contests. These permit a close look at how journalists perform nationwide—in Lufkin, Texas, as well as Long Island and Los Angeles, in Winston-Salem, North Carolina, and Willoughby, Ohio, as well as Washington, D.C. Our picture of media and politics is drawn recognizing recent structural changes in the electoral scene.

---

*The norms or regularities that we note may not stretch beyond this specific reportorial situation. But our discoveries are sufficiently disturbing to provoke similar inquiries directed at other levels of press performance.

Specifically, our view of press performance is framed by the following areas of inquiry:

How do reporters' newsgathering strategies affect how much they know about the candidacies and the amount of copy they produce for news columns? How are coverage patterns related to newspapers' resources (e.g., effort by the reporter) and candidates' resources (e.g., tenure in office or size of campaign war chest)?

Does reporters' selectivity in choosing facts and events mediate between messages promoted on the campaign trail and copy appearing in news articles? Does the journalistic community magnify some components of political communication and discount others? How does this translation process—from candidate, through reporters, and into news columns—affect voters' ability to make reasoned choices at the polls?

How does news attention vary with the competitiveness of a race? Are incumbents and challengers treated similarly? Are certain types of information more likely to appear for one candidate than another?

What is the style and language of newspaper editorials? What are the steps by which endorsement decisions are reached? Which staff members are involved in the choice of candidate? How does news coverage fit with endorsement preference?

What do the voters know about congressional contenders? How do these impressions link to the way they vote? Does the public consider candidates' stands on issues? How does press coverage compare with partisan advertising in creating voters' impressions of candidates? Do open races differ from the more typical contests between incumbents and challengers?

For our concluding chapter, we shared our research findings with journalists, candidates, and campaign aides, asking three broad questions:

Do our findings seem accountable? Are our interpretations familiar or fanciful?

How do you explain what we have found?

Have you any recommendations for how journalists and campaigners can undertake their tasks, improving press practices and encouraging competition for office?

Their suggestions are practical: the focus is on ways to work within the existing political system.

And the system depends on informed journalistic performance, as the results of our inquiry confirm. The way the press covers campaigns makes a difference in voters' understanding, in their opportunities to choose among candidates. But we come away from our surveys and personal encounters dubious about the tendency to cast journalists as activists—either as muckrakers, hounding officials and bureaucrats, or as conspirators, trying to exalt one candidate over another. Cases are probably rare where reporters lock arms with the editorial page in a conscious effort at propaganda.

More commonly, journalists covering campaigns seek routine ways to handle nonroutine news. They want to simplify and regularize their work load. Given a choice, they stick to the most accessible ways to gather news and avoid complex information. Like other occupations, newspaper work is more habitual than innovative. Habits favor the status quo—incumbents more than challengers—and weaken Congress's public accountability.

Many campaign reporters are young and have limited experience analyzing politics. Many hope fervently to escape the electoral beat for lusher journalistic pastures; their professional advancement requires continuous visibility and important or engaging stories.

We confess our prejudice at the outset: competition for public office seems desirable to us. There is precious little of that in the House elections, in the short run at least. Incumbents may feel nervous about their security in office, and may defer to the wishes of the public or the desires of Political Action Committees that fund them. But genuine opportunities to "turn the rascals out" are rare. And the content of press coverage provides a meager base for fueling vigorous public debate.

We cannot prove (1) that Congress's policy-making role would be strengthened by more hotly contested races for office; or (2) that more press attention to challengers is either deserved or necessary. But we think both propositions are true.

A word of caution is in order. Though some readers may wish to disregard our values or the implications we draw from our findings, the results should not be discounted on at least one ground. They are based on the first representative nationwide sample of political journalism ever assembled. But representativeness of findings may frustrate the unwary reader. Averages report typical journalistic and editorial activity in different electoral situations. Those who have worked on a congressional campaign may find that their personal experiences deviate from the general picture we draw. The particular and personal often depart from norms, a major argument in favor of gathering evidence from a cross section of events.

Our tale starts where others have left off. The journalist has not gone unstudied. Nor have media effects on political outcomes been neglected by the scholarly community.

Traditional Studies

The intersection of media and politics has most often found its expression in an analysis of electoral behavior in presidential elections. Unfortunately, this specialty has diverted attention from both news organizations and contests at lower levels. Furthermore, much of the research on journalistic habits concentrates on an elite corps, such as foreign correspondents (Cohen 1963) or Washington correspondents (Rosten 1937; Nimmo 1964; Miller 1978; Hess 1981a, 1981b). Another limitation arises from reliance on evidence that is merely anecdotal (e.g., Crouse 1973; Thompson 1973) or at least highly selective (e.g., Bernstein & Woodward 1974) instead of representative surveys of the press. Even the national portrait by Johnstone, Slawski, and Bowman (1976) fails to shed light on newsgathering patterns, nor does it link reportorial behavior to outcomes in news columns or broadcasts.

Though spinning yarns about investigative exploits may produce best-sellers, a price is paid in the misshapen view one gets of journalistic enterprise and in the propagation of widely shared myths concerning press practices. We descend from the lofty plane of presidential politics, where reporters attract almost as much commentary as candidates. Congressional campaigns are local, recurring events; as such, they provide an opportunity to uncover the more usual ingredients of political reporting. Media research into presidential campaigns exaggerates the level of public interest and of journalistic attentiveness to civic affairs.

During the last two decades, changes in the political scene have revised our view of campaign communication. The extent to which the media exert leverage, the processes by which this happens, and the ramifications of media effects on the political system are all being reconsidered (O'Keefe & Atwood 1981). It is small wonder that findings from the vintage campaign studies of the 1940's and 1950's have little applicability today.

Though popular opinion has always regarded the media as potent, the research community has been fickle in its view. The history of theories about media effects on voting fluctuates from images of massive influence, to limited effects, to powerful outcomes under certain conditions.

Following the First World War, the confluence of two themes helped establish the image of a mighty press. For one thing, growth in the size and complexity of society justified journalism's vital role: "The world that we have to deal with politically is out of reach, out of sight, out of mind. It has to be explored, reported, and imagined" (Lippmann 1922: 18). At the same time, psychological principles of learning through repetition surfaced in both popular and scholarly thinking. The result: propaganda and persuasion became synonymous. Finally, there was abundant "proof": Nazi Germany spawned horrifying examples, and even entertainment programs on radio (e.g., Orson Welles's "War of the Worlds" and daytime serials) were found to have sweeping influence.

The belief in the power of the press was severely undermined during the late 1940's and the 1950's. Two publications marked the watershed; both suggested that media effects are limited by selective screening mechanisms and interpersonal contacts.

The first blow was struck by Lazarsfeld, Berelson, and Gaudet in *The People's Choice* (1948), an examination of media patterns and vote decisions during the 1940 election. These researchers expected to find that political information exerts a strong impact on the electorate. Surprised by evidence of weak effects, the authors recast mass media as agents of reinforcement rather than change; evidently audience members had selectively exposed themselves to communication that was in accord with their previous beliefs. Though findings about selective exposure were slim, if statistically significant, the plausibility of this explanation generated widespread acceptance. The criterion by which media outcomes were evaluated was no longer conversion, but rather crystallization.

Klapper (1960) launched an even broader attack in his synthesis of communication research. He concluded that selective exposure had empirical support, though he cited only four studies. Another view now became popular, the one that mass communication does not ordinarily serve as a necessary and sufficient cause of audience effects, but functions between and through a nexus of mediating factors. This approach dominated during the 1950's and 1960's, despite its lack of methodological sophistication and a dearth of fresh evidence from the post-television era (McLeod & Reeves 1980).

The early 1970's saw a return to the notion of the power of the media, in part because of a retooling of research questions (Noelle-Neumann 1973). Calls for fresh approaches (e.g., Clarke & Kline 1974; Chaffee 1977) portend a more realistic understanding of mass media influence. Attitudinal or behavioral shifts are no longer the only interesting or even the most likely outcomes of media exposure. What people learn from the press and from other forms of communication currently attracts a lively interest.

Media and politics research now takes place in a broad setting. Voting behavior still attracts major attention; but even here, models of direct impact are being revised to include contextual features of media environment and of production constraints. Studies of other topics—the nature of news organizations, government controls on media, and the use of media by elites—are also beginning to appear.

The Context of Press Performance

Most previous research has failed to acknowledge the context in which events occur. The analysis of messages and audience behavior has found a comfortable niche among students of communication. Political science is appropriately concerned with only certain aspects of the electoral process—partisan defection rates and the conditions under which incumbents are defeated, for example.

The study of messages apart from the sources producing them or from the political leanings of those who receive them crowds events into a narrow aperture. Similarly, an examination of political systems without regard to communication vehicles is likely to yield less than satisfying results. Separatism robs both disciplines of explanatory power.

Though our study concentrates on press performance, allowances are made for changes in today's tessellated political landscape—redefined roles for parties, the emergence of Political Action Committees (PACs) and their well-filled coffers, rising campaign expenditures, and declining electoral participation. These changes reach dramatic sweep with the tide of campaign reforms crafted by the parties and Congress in the 1970's (Ranney 1979). We enter the 1980's with a transformed set of campaign rules that magnify the role of mass media.

Polsby (1980) recognizes the new communication order when he points out that "the principal mechanisms through which candidates and their enthusiasts exercise their power are the mass media of news dissemination." He agrees with others who suspect that a major effect of party reforms and legal change has been to supplant internal communication within political organizations with various forms of public communication. Polsby also draws attention to the importance of studying "work ways of the news media," because elites in this sector have joined, and sometimes replaced, party loyalists as the merchandisers of political influence (p. 55).

Rising campaign expenses also figure in the electoral revolution, and again the U.S. House presents a dramatic example. In 1978, first-time winners spent nearly one-quarter of a million dollars on average. Total campaign costs increased 44 percent between 1976 and 1978 (*Congressional Quarterly Weekly Report* 1979). The press's influence on the voter must be gauged alongside the impact of professional campaigning these monies can buy.

An industry has blossomed to help candidates cope with this new environment. Direct-mail consultants perfect fundraising techniques; the number of pollsters monitoring the public pulse expands; media advisers craft strategies to bypass organized political machinery and communicate directly with mass publics, even in the early stages of candidate winnowing.

Though many of the changes in candidate recruitment and financing were initiated at the presidential level, their effects have inevitably percolated to races for the U.S. House of Representatives. PACs have found these contests fertile ground for influence that is less effectively exerted elsewhere. New political styles have diffused beyond the presidency—in part because of weakened party structures and their lack of authority in the allocating of political patronage. PACs are increasingly important in fueling electoral strategies. In 1978, PACs accounted for 25 percent of congressional campaign costs; two years later the figure reached 35 percent (*Congressional Quarterly Weekly Report* 1980).

The looming role of PACs deserves special attention because it combines with trends in the press: politics and newspapers are becoming continental in management outlook—in "ownership" if you will. PAC money comes into congressional districts from outside sources, substituting for local support. A gradual nationalization of the House cannot help but result. At the same time, newspapers are nationalizing through chain ownership. Editors and publishers for Gannett and other groups look for career advancement through mobility; they want to move to larger markets and better salaries. Their stopover in middle-town America is often too short to permit a real understanding of local issues and concerns.

We suspect (but cannot demonstrate here) that a national

vocabulary about politics increasingly smooths over the rough corners of localism; outside money and a transient press play a more and more dominant role in electoral communication. This vocabulary naturally centers on the personal side of campaigns, on the candidates' political background and image. Issues, ties to voting blocs, and other quirks with local import can be expected to recede.

The forces at work in congressional races have had a marked impact on the political fortunes of our representatives. Since 1960, the success rate for House members seeking reelection has remained near 95 percent. By contrast, the success rate for incumbent senators has declined from that level to 60 percent. Members of the lower chamber, who serve shorter terms, now lead a more secure political life.

House composition is not only stable, it is maintained by lopsided votes. In the races we studied, incumbent/challenger contests were settled by an average vote margin of 36 percent; the outcomes of open races showed 24 percent spreads.

Along with these developments, voters show loosening ties to traditional political moorings; more people identify themselves as independents and refuse to vote straight tickets. Citizen participation has plunged; one of the more depressed rates can be found in elections to the U.S. House. In 1978, a postwar low was reached for off-years when only 35 percent of the eligible voters cast ballots.

To date, most observers have limited their views about political competition for office to fairly standard variables, ignoring the role of the press and other media. Studies have churned through the most obvious sources of incumbency advantage—control of redistricting, more intensive use of the perquisites of office, altered congressional functions (from policymaker to caseworker), shifts in voting behavior, and most recently, contenders' ability to attract money and organize effective campaigns. Access to news columns has been largely overlooked (for one exception, see M. Robinson 1981).

Methods

This survey of journalists was coordinated with the 1978 National Election Study (NES) sample of eligible voters (ICPSR 1979). We examine newspaper journalism and not broadcast reporting because print is where the coverage is; radio and television news, with signals that seldom match district boundaries, usually ignores congressional politicking.*

Our study does not include maneuvering during the primary season, but embraces only the general election period. We do not doubt the importance of the preliminary rounds. We wanted full data about press performance and voters' behavior; limited research resources forced our attention to the final six weeks of campaigning.

The design called for selecting one-quarter of the congressional districts in the continental United States. These 432 districts were partitioned into 108 strata, each containing four districts with comparable characteristics—geographical area, urbanization, and recent voting behavior. From each stratum, one district was drawn randomly. Of the 108 sample districts, 86 had races in which both major parties had candidates on the ballot. Our study was conducted in these contested districts. For each district, the newspaper with the largest daily circulation was chosen as an interview site.

The results are based on responses from 82 political reporters.† Seventy-one of these covered the most common type of race—involving incumbents seeking reelection—our principal concern. The other 11 covered open contests where the incumbent had been defeated in the primary, had retired, or was seeking election to some other office; these races are discussed in Chapter Six.

---

*The candidates of course use broadcast media for campaign advertising. This subject is taken up in Chapter Six.

†The three New York City newspapers were on strike during the pre-election period and were not included; and one reporter refused to be interviewed. This high response rate is only one sign of our interviewing success. Though these journalists were contacted in the rush of final campaign coverage, they bent over backward to help. Several had to interrupt our call to handle breaking news; all arranged later, more convenient times to continue the interview. Many volunteered information beyond the questions we asked; others asked for copies of our reports. The respondents' enthusiasm and openness were confirmed by our follow-up conversations, leading to Chapter Seven. Journalists tend to provide the fullest details about their work when open-ended questions recognize the realities of their roles and invite answers that vary in length. Our interviewers were periodically debriefed as field work progressed. They found the group's eagerness remarkable compared with other groups they had surveyed.

Through phone contacts with each paper, we identified the political reporter assigned to cover our selected congressional race.* During the two weeks prior to the election, interviews lasting 40–60 minutes were conducted by trained staff at Michigan's Survey Research Center.

In addition to the survey data, newspapers were collected from all sites where reporter interviews had taken place. News stories, editorials, opinion columns, advertisements, and letters were clipped from September 27 through Election Day, November 7. This analysis examines news articles and editorials. Coding guidelines called for the inclusion of each of the 5,183 paragraphs (in 731 articles) in which a candidate's name or a reference to the candidate appeared. More than one mention in a paragraph was treated as a single mention. Name mention and paragraph mention are used interchangeably throughout this study. Within each paragraph, we coded the presence or absence of each of five content themes of political communication.† The scheme separately links incumbents and challengers to copy specifically associated with them.‡

* We expected that the political reporter interviewed would satisfactorily represent the newspaper's coverage of the congressional race. As reassurance we asked, "Are there any other reporters at your paper who help cover the (named) District campaign?" The correlation between our designated respondent's journalistic activity and the number of times the candidates' names appeared does not vary between newspapers with one or more than one reporter. This confirms that our primary respondent at each site adequately represented the paper's coverage.

† Three coders averaged 91 percent agreement in assigning the content codes to individual paragraphs. Stories were coded according to seven themes of information that could be associated with candidates; analysis has collapsed them to five: political attributes, personal characteristics, issue stands/ideology/group ties, party affiliation, and features of campaign organization. Examples and an analysis of the themes are given in Chapter Three.

‡ This research required the merging of data from surveys with newspaper materials and pertinent published sources, and necessitated a sophisticated management of computer software. We are grateful to Peter Joftis for his advice and problem solving at this stage of the inquiry.

II

Reporters on the Campaign Trail

REPORTERS bring tricks of the trade, proven ways for gathering news, to their political assignments. Our study shows that the more techniques they use, the more they know about the candidates and the greater news space they succeed in capturing for campaign stories.

But this labor pays different dividends for incumbents and challengers; furthermore, some ways of gathering news are more fruitful than others. We inspect reporters' routines to answer three questions. Which sources do journalists tap for information? Which strategies teach the reporters the most? What is the harvest of news copy from reporting effort? On the basis of the answers, one can judge whether journalists work diligently to gather information or lazily depend on handouts for their daily diet of campaign coverage.

We dig into the mechanics of newsgathering, rather than just looking at the number of articles appearing in papers (see, e.g., Graber 1971). First, we examine the wide range of newsgathering tasks and information sources available to local political reporters. We consider both passive channels (such as the receipt of press releases) and those requiring considerably more vigor and imagination (such as contacting local community groups).

Reportorial methods are combined into an activity index that predicts two outcomes: (1) how much reporters know about campaigns, and (2) the quantity of news copy appearing in print.

Studies of Newsgathering

The first systematic inquiry into newsgathering practices (Rosten 1937) focused on Washington correspondents and their sources. Even though press releases, conferences, and handouts were widely used, Rosten acknowledged that "the correspondent who wished information of a more revealing nature is obliged to cultivate private news sources" (p. 78).

Revisionists have emphasized institutional arrangements and their influence on patterns of press contacts. Sigal (1973), in his penetrating analysis of the *Washington Post* and the *New York Times*, uncovered organizational routines and policies that affected the way news was gathered and the shape of news content. He was interested primarily in how choices made through the chain of command meshed with bureaucratic requirements of the news operation. Systems of newsgathering explained more about news content than the political proclivities of individual journalists did. In short, "What newspeople report may depend less on who they are than on how they work" (p. 5).

Sigal sorted news channels, "the paths by which information reaches a reporter" (p. 120), into three broad categories. Routine channels—official proceedings, press releases, press conferences, and nonspontaneous events such as speeches, ceremonies, and staged demonstrations—accounted for more than half of the stories. Enterprise channels, consisting primarily of interviews conducted at the reporter's initiative, but also including spontaneous events the reporter witnessed firsthand, research from documents and books, and the reporter's own conclusions and analysis, contributed about a quarter. The third information channel was informal and consisted of background briefings, leaks, nongovernment proceedings, news reports from other news organizations, interviews with reporters, and editorials.

Tunstall (1971) took a close look at the newsgathering activities of British correspondents who specialized in politics, aviation, education, labor, crime, football, fashion, and motoring. The lore of journalism holds that people make news, and fully two-thirds of Tunstall's reporters thought that individuals were more important sources than organizations.

Consistent with this belief, specialists spent most of their time talking—in face-to-face meetings, in community gatherings, and on the telephone. Political writers frequently dealt with documents, but this was almost always in conjunction with personal encounters. Tunstall reached the same conclusion as Rosten did in his study of Washington correspondents—that newspeople use printed materials as a basic resource, but an "effective specialist is largely defined as a person who is on personal terms with important persons in the relevant field" (Tunstall 1971: 160).

The interaction between newsgatherer and source was the focus of Nimmo's (1964) study. He discussed the preferences, of both reporters and public information officers, for newsgathering methods. The reporters' first choice as a means of acquiring information was the interview. Almost all said personal contact was "invaluable" and cited advantages: provides a peg for a story, increases story interest, lends topicality, provides exclusive information, and allows the reporter to stay ahead of the competition. News conferences, the reporters' second choice, came under considerable criticism because of the mass atmosphere and the nonexclusive and largely propagandistic information provided. Reporters lavished no praise on news releases; nevertheless, they used them with some regularity.

Congressional Coverage

The institution of Congress, blending the power of decision with parochial roots, lacks much of the journalistic glamour of the executive office. But covering the Hill and its occupants has attracted scrutiny by experienced newspersons and other analysts. Their accounts can leave one confused about the visibility of the congressional stage.

Cannon (1977: 181–82, 190) points to a retreat by House members from public view:

Despite the impressiveness of the numbers, most newspapers in the country simply have no congressional coverage they can call their own. This is fine with most congressmen. Among the various high crimes and misdemeanors with which they charge the press, noncoverage is not one of them.

Between the big story and the local sewer grant lies a vast under-reported landscape of congressional achievements, scandals, and intrigue which is almost never seen in the daily paper, let alone on local television. In this wasteland, a symbiotic relationship flourishes between congressmen and correspondent, a relationship based on mutual need and sometimes on mutual laziness. This relationship permits the typical invisible congressman to become visible in a highly selective way in his home district.

Congressional correspondents were once at the top of the heap in Washington, occupying the place taken over successively by White House correspondents and foreign correspondents and now by investigative reporters. . . . It is no accident that in four decades of retreat and acquiescence by Congress to the claims of the executive branch the press developed a preoccupation—some would say an obsession—with the presidency. Nor is it any accident that Congress, in the wake of the impeachment inquiry and subsequent resurgence of the Democratic caucus, is becoming the focal point for coverage again. "As it was perceived that the Congress and particularly the House of Representatives was losing power, it tended also to lose visibility," says David Broder.

Nonetheless, congressional news acquires a special tempo during elections, rooted in the politician's mythical ability to capture attention. Roshco (1975: 73) observes:

Politics is the most complex, elusive, and socially consequential of the dramaturgic news beats. Therefore, it most deeply illustrates fundamental aspects of newsmaking. High public visibility is as characteristic of the status of being an elected official as of being an athlete or actor. Assuring his visibility to appropriate audiences is basic to a politician's role-performance, and efforts to gain and maintain this visibility underlie much political news. . . . On most other beats, for which crime reporting can be taken as a prototype, reporters usually must wait to be alerted to breaks in taken-for-granted routines. . . . Politics, on the other hand, is preeminently a beat on which daily role-performance tends to be newsworthy.

But the "newsworthiness" of actors on the political stage varies considerably. Most scholars agree with Sigal (1973: 127), that the boom in executive coverage has been accompanied by waning attention to the House:

The combination of the beat system and reporter reliance on routine channels has affected the ability of the Members of Congress to make news. As the beat system has expanded over time, relatively fewer correspondents on the *Times* and the *Post* are assigned to the Capitol Hill beat. Legislators in pivotal positions in Congress have become more adept at disseminating information to the press, releasing reports on Saturday for Sunday papers, issuing press releases, and in general making themselves more available to reporters. . . . However adept they have become at using the press, Congressmen have not kept pace with the expansion of the newsmaking capabilities in the Executive Branch. The consequence has been a decline over time in the proportion of Congressmen among official news sources for page-one stories in the *Times* and the *Post*.

And as Cannon (1977: 179) notes, "Politicians who 'graduate' to the House of Representatives from a modern legislature often are surprised to find that they have left a highly visible forum for an almost invisible one."

We argue that congressional campaign reporting deserves particular scrutiny because it helps gauge the quality of press performance nationally. All newspapers, at least in contested districts, have a stake in informing the public. Though the voters' sense of involvement may have slipped to a new low in recent years, their lives are inescapably affected, at the local level as well as the national level, by congressional action. The race for office provides a setting in which to study routine ingredients of sound political coverage.

Popular accounts (e.g., Crouse 1973) have documented folkways of the press that lead to inaccurate or narrow political journalism on the national scene. Few of these barriers plague local newspeople. "Packs" are small or nonexistent; the legitimizing influence of "elite" papers rarely intervenes. Local reporters seldom dog the steps of congressional candidates or develop the kinds of close relationships that blossom between journalists and presidential contenders as they slog through state primaries together. These journalists are not bound by habits found in highly competitive journalistic enterprise.

Elections to the House bring members and other candidates into close interaction with media. But we should not expect uniform results. Districts range in size from a handful of city blocks to an entire state. News outlets covering these widely differing zones are similarly diverse.

Except for the final weeks of the campaign, one major source of information, the incumbent, is not continuously in the district. He or she must be represented by surrogates or must feed news from Washington. An incumbent's urgency about satisfying press appetites surely depends on how threatened he or she feels. A challenger's ability to mobilize press attention hinges on skill and resources, chiefly money.

Most news organizations in our sample engage in some planning before the general election, and about a third reassign reporters from different beats and responsibilities. A number of different patterns for allocating staff emerge. At some newspapers, a single reporter covers several congressional races. At others, these elections are part of a government, city hall, county, or state beat.

About half of our respondents consider themselves full-time political reporters; half are spread between politics and other beats. None of these journalists devotes complete attention to our chosen congressional race. In fact, most reporters spend less than 15 percent of their election-period time covering the district we chose to study; half split responsibility for campaign coverage with at least one other reporter.

Newsgathering Techniques

Classification schemes, including Rosten's seminal analysis (1937), regularly uncover two dimensions of newsgathering. One characterizes reporters' activeness or passiveness; the other describes the source of information, personal contacts or impersonal documents. From our interviews we identified 12 classes of newsgathering techniques as shown in Table 1. Some activities were asked separately for each contender, others were not candidate-specific. The exact wording of the questions and a breakdown of the responses appear in Appendix A. We consider a technique active if it requires initiative in seeking out news events and stories: interviewing candidates and sources close to them, for instance. Passive techniques, making minimal demands on the reporter, are those in which information flows onto the reporter's desk. Receipt of news releases and use of wire copy are but two examples.

Active-personal. Curiously, the technique of going directly to a public figure as a news source did not become a part of

TABLE 1
Types of Newsgathering Techniques

Character of reporter's work	Technique
Active-personal	Interview candidate
	Talk to manager
	Interview endorsing groups
	Attend press conference
	Attend speeches
	Other activities (polls, investigations, etc.)
Passive-impersonal	Receive news releases
	Receive speech drafts
	Use wire copy
	Read other papers
Active-impersonal	Research in other sources
Passive-personal	Talk to other reporters

political journalism until the 1860's (Schudson 1978). Since then, of course, it has become routine. Our reporters were asked if they had interviewed or talked personally with the candidates during the election period and, if so, how often this had happened. Direct contact with both the incumbent and the challenger was common; 80 percent interviewed each contender at least once, and half claim to have had contact four or more times.

Interviews come in two varieties: planned by reporters and instigated by other forces, sometimes accidental. Half of our journalists say that they set up all their interviews; the rest concede some initiative on the part of candidates or their aides. Sometimes encounters seem "just to happen," either at the newspaper or at some public event. As Hohenberg (1960: 253) explains, often reporters and sources "happen to meet on the street, or at a luncheon or cocktail party, or they have a casual exchange over a drink in the late afternoon."

We should not overlook the fact that adroit press aides make a specialty of subtly arranging accidental meetings. And we know from studies in psychology as well as from personal experience that unpremeditated encounters often contain more potential for persuasion than carefully planned events. Though an interesting test of the political sophistication of reporters might explore how they made contact with their sources, our questions did not probe this deeply.

Another strategy in political journalism is to contact those closest to the campaign organization, for instance the manager. In 1976 the pollster Peter Hart characterized most House campaigns as Mom-and-Pop efforts, low on money and professionalism (*Congressional Quarterly Weekly Report* 1977). His observation was based on survey results indicating that only 27 percent of House campaigns had salaried campaign managers, and fewer still employed paid accountants, treasurers, or lawyers.

Since then, however, the growing sophistication of congressional races has been mirrored in campaign expenditures that have increased dramatically over the past few elections.* The use of campaign managers has increased accordingly. Our definition of manager includes the novice and the seasoned professional; in 1978, two-thirds of the candidates employed such personnel. About 60 percent of the reporters talked to at least one of the managers; as we shall see, the payoff from this encounter is consequential.

Representatives exhibit different "home styles" (Fenno 1978) that are understandable in light of perceived constituencies. But rank-and-file voters are not the sum of the constituency. Candidates for office respond to demands from interest groups, political elites, party leaders, and others. Supporting coalitions "provide finances and campaign workers, and, to an extent, contribute their influence with certain voters—all of which help the candidate in his attempt to gain office" (Kingdon 1966: 45). About half of our journalists contacted politically active forces in the district—people or groups who support or endorse one of the candidates—and identified their source in our interviews.

*The mean expenditures for challengers across four elections—1974, 1976, 1978, and 1980—moved from $40,000 to $51,000 to $72,000 to $100,000. The comparable figures for incumbents were $56,000, $79,000, $112,000, and $165,000. Candidates for open seats far outspent the others—$90,000, $125,000, $201,000, and $209,000. (Ornstein et al. 1982.)

Press conferences and speeches before local organizations combine initiative on the part of both reporters and contenders. Press conferences, at least in these contested races, were not particularly popular. Fewer than half of the candidates even held these events; and if they did, reporters tended to cover all or none of them.

As one journalism text notes, "Very little happens at a news conference that is not anticipated in some way . . . and reporters fully realize, when they ask questions . . . that they are making news for their competitors as well as for themselves" (Hohenberg 1960: 251–52). Washington correspondents criticize the events for precisely this reason—the non-exclusive nature of the material unearthed (Nimmo 1964). It appears that press conferences are risky events for both candidates and the press. They are scheduled in advance for the convenience of the media—thus heralding major announcements. Low turnout could blight the significance of the event. It is no wonder that candidates are reluctant to stage these happenings, where only habitués may appear. And it comes as no surprise that reporters are more likely to engage in activities that promise some return for the investment of time.

Speeches before various civic, interest, and professional groups are a staple of campaigning. Almost all of the candidates do this. But few members of the local press corps cover these engagements. If the press did attend, candidates might face a conflict between the need to cement votes and the need to say something novel for press consumption. But for the most part, from the reporter's point of view these routine luncheons and dinners are burdensome, redundant, and unlikely to produce much newsworthy copy.

Reporters were asked whether they had done anything else to cover campaigns and candidates. About half said yes, citing in-depth stories or candidate profiles written to supplement routine coverage.* Examples of such activities are:

---

*Most of the responses to this question involved personal contacts. Only a sprinkling of impersonal activities appeared (for example, "I've gone over statistics of past campaigns, how he ran in different parts of the district"). In a few cases, it could not be determined whether the reporter's additional efforts were of a personal or an impersonal character.

"I spent several days with each of the candidates."

"We've run a month-long series entitled 'The Candidates Speak'—in this we've developed a series of issues that we've thought to be important and then have solicited written responses from candidates, which are then published twice weekly."

"I'm conducting a poll before the election."

"I did a week-long investigation of his finances."

"I've talked to other politicians to see who they are supporting."

"Talked to campaign workers and read their literature."

"Talked to key staffers, both in D.C. and locally."

"I get out and talk to voters about how they feel."

"I talked to state party people."

Passive-impersonal. Press releases, drafts of speeches, position papers, and campaign literature are unsolicited sources of information that cascade onto the reporter's desk. Releases, for instance, are often issued on a daily basis during the final weeks of campaigning. Their use has been the subject of considerably more commentary and speculation than direct scrutiny. Discussing Capitol Hill's publicists, Bagdikian (1974: 4) says, "Most of the media are willing conduits for the highly selective information the members of Congress decide to feed the electorate. This propaganda is sent to newspapers and broadcasting stations, and the vast majority of them pass it off to the voters as professionally collected, written, and edited 'news.'"

However, a study of the use of releases by weekly newspapers in a nonelection year (Polk, Eddy & Andre 1975) found "very low efficiency rates" for the publicist. Use was modest, given the number and length of the releases issued. And there was little support for the assertion that releases are published verbatim. These authors concluded that "officeholders are minimally successful in mailings to weekly newspapers. . . . Editors are not so gullible and do not passively accept Capitol Hill releases" (p. 546).

Three scholars have studied the fate of releases prepared by candidates seeking elective office. Kaid (1976) found that state senate candidates did not generate much news copy from releases. But when she compared this low response with the amount of copy given to contestants who did not issue press statements at all, releases were shown to increase coverage threefold.

Candidates in a New Jersey gubernatorial race (Vermeer 1978) issued about one release a day. Though neither efficiency nor utilization rates were computed, the author concluded that "if the volume of releases is any indication, campaign news releases can be an important source of news for the press, especially for those papers which cannot assign a reporter to cover the campaign full-time" (p. 16).

Atwood (1980) reached much the same conclusion, judging that newspaper editors relied heavily on congressional candidates' press releases for campaign coverage. But he also noted that much of the material in the releases and in the news stories focused on noncandidate topics, a finding that differs from most previous research. As Dunn (1969: 40) noted, in his study of public officials and the press, reporters recognize the self-serving nature of releases, yet acknowledge their usefulness in "providing more information than they would otherwise have."

As can be seen, agreement about the effectiveness of releases is hard to reach. And no wonder. Though a release might fail to be copied as a news story, the information it contains may channel reporters' energies, leading them toward stories the candidate favors or whetting their investigative appetites.

Our interviews with reporters covered too many topics for us to settle the questions about the impacts of news releases. Most of our journalists receive releases and at least scan them. Often the content is redundant or includes announcements of speaking engagements and appearances. Many of our journalists expressed concern about becoming vehicles for the campaign line.

Candidates commonly supply drafts of speeches and position papers. Over half of our respondents read these. Attention to wire-service stories is less frequent. After the exodus from Washington, during the final three weeks of the campaign, news is generated from events within the district. The newspaper's state or Washington bureau does not contribute much to House campaign coverage.

Reading newspapers is an important, if passive, news-gathering technique. Accounts of journalism (e.g., Johnstone, Slawski & Bowman 1976) often focus on the shared professional judgments that develop among beat reporters as a result of following each other's work. These values are cited as an explanation for the homogeneity of reportage across dissimilar organizational settings and political backdrops. Articles that colleagues draft become important cues for reporters (Rosten 1937; Cohen 1963; Rivers 1965).

This national sample includes districts with a wide array of coverage areas: districts embedded in metropolitan areas too large for complete congressional coverage, districts with considerable coincidence between the newspaper's circulation area and the district boundaries, districts where the circulation zone is but a small corner of the political area. Despite this variety in the delivery of campaign news, almost all newspeople read other papers' accounts of the races. These news columns appear not only in dailies, but in weekly newspapers circulating throughout the districts.

Active-impersonal. Journalists oftentimes incorporate some background information into their stories. Morgue files, the *Congressional Quarterly*, Federal Election Commission (FEC) reports,* and the like are consulted for documenting legislative initiative and action, electoral trends, district demographics, and biographical facts on the candidates. About 60 percent of the journalists used "the public library or reference sources to find out things about the candidates or their campaigns."

Passive-personal. Professional colleagues are an obvious, if overlooked, source of information. Hess (1981b) contends

---

*Candidates must report campaign receipts and expenditures to the Federal Election Commission. Itemized expenditures are included on Schedule B forms, and require name of payee, purpose of expenditure, date, and exact amount of payment. Disbursements cover office expenses, staff salaries, financial transactions, research, individual and organized campaign events, advertising, and media purchases.

that the isolation of reporters from both consumers and their own managements contributes to their seeking rewards from association with their colleagues. The sociologist Robert Darnton, recalling his days on the *New York Times*, says: "We really wrote for one another. Our primary reference group was spread around us in the newsroom" (quoted in Hess 1981b). Nearly two-thirds of our journalists talked with reporters from their own paper and from other papers.

Effects of Journalistic Effort

Our attention is drawn to the results of these newsgathering tasks. At a minimum, applying more time and energy should enrich reporters' understanding and sophistication about candidates and their campaigns. We examine how reporters' techniques differ in terms of one key outcome: knowledge about the campaigns. Reporters were asked: *Regardless of what the candidates are emphasizing, I'd like to ask what you feel are the strengths and weaknesses in the candidates' campaigns. What are (Candidate A's/B's) strengths? What are (Candidate A's/B's) weaknesses?* Journalists offered, on average, seven mentions for each candidate. Information-holding, separately for incumbents and for challengers, was constructed by summing the number of individual strengths and weaknesses mentioned.*

Newsgathering activities—effort spent following congressional campaigns—account for much of reporters' repertoire of analytic commentary, especially for challengers. The 12 activities were run in a multiple regression predicting the number of strengths and weaknesses known, separately for incumbents and challengers. This disclosed that reporters get more of their information on challengers from these activities ($r^2 = .55$) than they get for incumbents ($r^2 = .43$). That result is not surprising. Years in office provide many reporters with a solid base of knowledge about incumbents. Much

---

*Throughout this analysis we compare incumbents and challengers. This departs from a research tradition in which scholars studying congressional elections have been preoccupied with the explanatory power of party identification (e.g., Stokes & Miller 1966). More recent analyses offer strong support for models that include the advantages of incumbency (Mayhew 1974; Cover 1977; Ferejohn 1977). Our analysis confirms this point.

of the lore echoes anecdotes and impressions from previous forays into the congressional fray. But challengers are relatively new actors on the political stage. Work—seeking, digging, reading, phoning, asking, talking—is responsible for many of the reporters' notions about these contenders.

Information is gained through a variety of channels, each of which can be characterized by the dividends it pays. Are certain newsgathering techniques more productive than others? Are incumbents and challengers covered differently? Before discussing particulars, let us note two major findings:

1. The ranking of effective newsgathering techniques is similar for incumbents and challengers.

2. Contact with the campaign manager is a particularly valuable information source.

Other students of media and politics (e.g. Rosten 1937; Nimmo 1964; Sigal 1973) have concluded that personal contacts are the most useful news sources. Table 2, which lists each reportorial activity ordered by its yield in journalists' information-holding, provides a bit of brute empirical evidence to fortify these earlier observations.

For both incumbents and challengers, active-personal techniques produce the best payoff. Of the other channels, only press releases contribute to the journalists' interpretive faculties. The disparate snippets of information—an issue stand, a speaking engagement, an endorsement—communicated through an incessant flow of releases, eventually find a niche in the reporter's storehouse of campaign knowledge.

Interviews with campaign managers rank even higher than candidate interviews in explaining how much reporters know about campaigns. This underscores the value of a successful fund-raising effort, especially in the early stages, for hiring the best talent available. Early staffing of the campaign, a natural advantage incumbents enjoy, can pay dividends in journalists' knowledgeability.

Interviews with endorsing groups or individuals is an effective technique, for both incumbents and challengers. But only half our reporters did this during the campaign. Even fewer regularly attended meetings where candidates spoke, another useful way to learn about the contenders, especially challengers.

TABLE 2
Ranking of Newsgathering Techniques,
by Effectiveness and Candidacy

Coverage of incumbents	Coverage of challengers
Talk to manager	Attend speeches
Other activities	Talk to manager
Interview candidate	Interview candidate
Receive news releases	Interview endorsing groups
Attend speeches	Receive news releases
Interview endorsing groups	Research in other sources
Research in other sources	Other activities
Receive speech drafts	Receive speech drafts
Attend press conferences	Talk to other reporters
Read other papers	Read other papers
Use wire copy	Attend press conferences
Talk to other reporters	Use wire copy

NOTE: The rankings reflect beta weights based on Multiple Classification Analysis (Andrews et al. 1975).

And so the bulk of the information reporters gain can be traced directly to the heart of campaigns, the candidate or his or her "handler." These most-accessible sources overshadow other avenues of inquiry that could cast a different light on the campaigns.

The least useful paths to gaining an understanding of the political scene are drafts of speeches, press conferences, wire-service accounts, reportage in other newspapers, and talking to other reporters. (However, those channels may be important for state or national contests.)

Our technique-by-technique analysis of what reporters know identifies the newsgathering methods that typically work best. But a further look at journalistic output requires a general index of reporting effort, one that takes all techniques into account. We coded the 12 newsgathering methods into the categories shown in Appendix A. Reporters received credit for each increase in frequency of activity; the summed score assigns equal weight to the various ways of gathering news.

We have already seen that journalistic effort leads to an ability to talk about the campaign in a detailed fashion. Yet journalism is more than a reservoir of impressions and opinions. Press performance must be judged not only by what reporters know—although this is an interesting halfway point— but by what they communicate in news columns.

We measured newspaper content by aggregating candidate name mentions that appeared in articles during the campaign period. The correlations between total mentions and each of our five content themes are very high. Though frequency of name is a gross measure, it is the best single representation we have for journalistic output.*

For the present, we want to depict the flow of campaign information from the stage of newsgathering to the appearance of stories in the paper. Of course, editors and other gatekeepers intervene; another report from our study (Clarke & Evans 1980) discloses how newsroom bureaucracy affects journalistic performance.

Our story asks two additional questions here, beyond reporters' understanding of the candidates. First, does the effort a journalist expends convert into news copy at the same rate for incumbents and challengers? The answer is yes. The relationship between reportorial work and the amount of copy appearing in news columns is strong and significant for both incumbents (rho = .56) and challengers (rho = .57). When our 71 reporters invested effort on the campaign trail, they had to show a return—for their own satisfaction, if not the newspaper's management.

Second, does this equality in news process yield equal news treatment? No, it does not, though this seems to defy logic. Chapter Four provides the most vivid evidence of how

*Davidson and Parker's (1972) data point to sheer media exposure as the largest correlate of the public's support for Congress, as measured by favorable evaluations of representatives' performance. The use of media outscores political participation, party affiliation, political efficacy, and other familiar variables in predictive power. The authors speculate: "Perhaps it is not the content of the media messages, but simply the fact of extensive coverage that elevates the standing of governmental institutions" (p. 610). This conjecture about the effects of the media in conferring status supports our use of paragraphs, or number of candidate references, as an index of journalistic output.

challengers struggle against a lower threshold of press attention than incumbents. Our explanation here takes on a different texture by examining the communication process in light of the resources that contenders bring to the campaign fray.

Effects of Candidates' Resources

Not all incumbents or all challengers are alike; some have greater advantages than others. What are the most significant resources that these two groups bring to the race?

For incumbents, we suggest that number of terms spent in office is the most important (Fenno 1978). As the years roll by, the incumbents' stands on the issues become widely known, their attendance and voting records are routinely covered, they are appointed to more powerful and prestigious committees, and they have acquired a fund of goodwill through constituent services.*

Challengers obviously must tap a different resource. What criterion distinguishes weak challengers from those who mount a realistic threat to sitting representatives? The answer is not hard to find: money. Recent analyses have examined the consequences of candidate spending on election outcomes. Controlling for national factors and party representation in the district, Jacobson (1978) found that the challenger's proportion of the two-party vote is very much a function of how much he or she spends—and the challenger spends as much as can be raised. In contrast, the incumbent's spending reacts to the spending level of his or her opponent, but without much success in affecting the vote. Candidate campaign activities and money make a difference, particularly for challengers and for contenders in open races.

When incumbents' resources are defined by the number of terms in office, a median split divides House members into those who have been in office from one to four terms (low resource) and those who have been in office five terms or

---

*Though length of service presumably confers skills in mounting election campaigns, longevity does not by itself lead to security in office. Erikson (1978) shows that an incumbent's chances of defeat are unaffected by the number of previous terms—at least in the middle range from two to a dozen.

more (high resource). For challengers, we cut FEC reports of total expenditures during the primary and general election campaign period at the median. This yields a low-resource group with median expenditures of $7,100 and a high-resource group with $65,000 on average.

We again look at conversion rates—the relationship between journalistic effort and published news copy. It is the challenger without money who suffers from journalistic inattention. For that unlucky contender, hard digging by the few reporters who exert themselves does not produce significantly more paragraphs of copy than are dished up by less enterprising newsgatherers. In all other candidacies—well-financed challengers and all incumbents—effort relates strongly and significantly with news output.*

The picture becomes even more clear when we examine each type of candidate's visibility in news columns. Table 3 presents median number of paragraph mentions for our four kinds of candidacies.

Underfinanced challengers stand out with a median of only five paragraphs in the news. Their case is even more forlorn because of the lack of correlation with reporting effort already noted. A few reporters did cover low-resource challengers with great energy. But even in these cases, the amount of copy they produced (median of 28 paragraphs) falls below the amount a well-financed challenger typically received (39 mentions). So even where newspapers exert peak energy following a low-budget challenger, that candidate's lack of resources continues to limit the amount of information that gets into print for public consumption.

A further look at Table 3 discloses an interesting difference between short-term and long-term incumbents. The former receive twice the play in news. In many cases, the relative invisibility of long-timers is hardly a liability to them, perhaps even a blessing; their reelection is assured, with few exceptions, and the campaign draws a yawning response from all quarters.

*The correlation between journalistic effort and news coverage is .59 for low-resource incumbents; .49 for high-resource incumbents; .30 (non-significant) for low-resource challengers; and .41 for high-resource challengers.

TABLE 3
Median Number of Paragraph Mentions,
by Candidacy and Resources

Group covered	No. of mentions	Group covered	No. of mentions
Incumbents		Challengers	
Low resources	44	Low resources	5
High resources	20	High resources	39

NOTE: For incumbents, resources are defined by the number of terms in office; a median split divides members into a low-resource group (1–4 terms) and a high-resource group (5 or more terms). For challengers, FEC reports of total expenditures during the primary and general election were cut at the median, yielding a low-resource group with media expenditures of $7,100 and a high-resource group with media expenditures of $65,000.

Discussion

One lesson from our analysis is stark: money is essential to fuel the challenger's campaign information machine. No amount of journalistic enterprise that we found by eager reporters compensates for the dead weight of invisibility that flows naturally from a lack of funds—to hire managers, schedule media events, and buy ads that help certify a contender's political legitimacy.

Earlier in the chapter we presented techniques of "typical" campaign reporting in full knowledge of how easily averages can mislead when offered to describe a highly variable activity.* Most political journalists assigned to a congressional race spend less than one in six work hours on it. No wonder that they pass over familiar and available news sources—politically active groups and archives or other banks of information. The dogged methods of an I. F. Stone are not frequently found on the congressional campaign trail. In one of five elections, neither of the candidates is contacted.

Conversations with campaign managers loom in importance. Though these personable and press-wise authorities

---

*And of course press activity is not the only variable; models attempting to explain the relationship between the press and politicians have focused on many other factors, including competitiveness and the importance of the election. For a discussion, see Blumler & Gurevitch 1981.

are not always employed by candidates, they are invaluable for educating reporters, and ultimately for gaining news play. Reporters learn more about candidates, and newspapers publish more, where experts are at hand to guide journalists on their way.

We offer a final speculation toward the building of a theory about press attention to candidacies. A supply-demand model may account in large part for effort or lack thereof by political reporters. They generally work hard when they know that usable copy can be easily mined. They slack off in the face of difficulty. Organizational efficiency mandates the least amount of selective editing possible. Candidacies judged difficult to report will lack coverage for that very reason, not because of a harsh editorial pencil.

More about the subtleties of news economics awaits another analysis. It would combine data about ways that some candidates make themselves accessible to the press, even when they are poorly financed. The study would ask whether contrived increases in the supply of potential news can whet journalists' demand for even more. Can the spiral that dooms so many challengers to invisibility be broken?

III

From Candidates to Copy

A JOURNALIST'S selective use of facts and events is shaped by professional standards of newsworthiness and expectations about audience interest. These discretionary filtering processes are the subject of this chapter. Specifically, we examine how reporters perceive, evaluate, and produce political information. We discover how their interpretation of contenders' campaigns affects the copy that appears in news articles. Our findings offer clues to what inhibits competitiveness in congressional elections. And this research highlights practices that might affect the voters' ability to make reasoned choices at the polls.

Studies of Media Selectivity

Two approaches have been used to examine how journalists' views influence their newswriting. One inquires into what reporters and editors carry to their work: values (Gieber 1964; Paletz, Reichert & McIntyre 1971), prior expectations (Lang & Lang 1953), states of cognitive tension (Greenberg & Tannenbaum 1962), or need fulfillment (Pool & Shulman 1959). This perspective has unearthed many, sometimes conflicting processes affecting grammatical accuracy, attributions of causality, and other semantic and syntactical features.

A second approach, pursued by sociologists with a qualitative bent, probes how institutional arrangements channel the coverage of events. Breed (1955) examines subtle bureaucratic controls operating within the newsroom. Tuchman (1972) focuses on "strategic rituals" that aid in processing the raw material reporters handle. Epstein (1973) alerts us to the "manufacturing" requirements of television news. Outside journalism, Cantor (1971; 1980) shows how work habits and contractual relationships in the television industry influence script materials and other artistic elements.

Professional standards, social controls, and systemic requirements notwithstanding, news articles are based in large part on the data-gathering reporters do and the analytic skills they bring to their assignments. News is not alone what reporters make it, but their closeness to sources makes them the most important figures in the dissemination of political information.

Our approach is diagnostic rather than strictly theoretical. We examine how information on congressional contests passes through the journalistic sieve on its way to the newspaper-reading public. Journalists make choices in their coverage, writing about or ignoring certain types of information on candidates. For purposes of this analysis, we categorize these into five content themes: political attributes; personal characteristics; issues/ideology/group ties; party affiliation; and campaign organization.

Separating these themes of how campaigns are reported serves another purpose. We have remarked the lack of political competition found in the races for the House since 1968. Perhaps reporters' practices help account for this stagnation (Kelley 1959), which can so easily lead to failures in accountability (Mintz & Cohen 1976). Stability in office, for example, may result from portrayals of incumbents that differ thematically from reporting about challengers. In short, the content as well as the volume of political information may help explain incumbents' iron grip on office and suggest the seeds of nonaccountability.

This chapter presents a detailed analysis of the way journalists perceive political races, judge the merits and liabilities of contenders, and write about campaigns. It also examines how the content of political reporting varies according to the types of candidates running and the resources they bring to the electoral fray.

Three Views of the Campaign

Three views of congressional campaigns are (1) the campaign as event, (2) the campaign as analyzed by journalists, and (3) the campaign as it appears in news articles.

The campaign as event. It is unwieldy to reconstruct 71 campaigns by means of independent observation, a powerful strategy used by Paletz and his colleagues (1971) in a single case study. Instead we queried journalists about their perceptions of the messages contenders were promoting on the campaign trail, the appeals used to gain votes. Interviewers asked: *I have some questions about the candidates and their campaigns. In terms of background, personal characteristics, and issues, what are the things (Candidate A/B) is emphasizing to the voters in the campaign? Any others?*

Reporters provided richly detailed accounts. These campaign *emphases* (hereafter called) were coded into 512 categories, later collapsed into the five major themes of political information.* Examples (including items more frequently mentioned as strengths and weaknesses) are:

1. Political attributes: experience in government, years in office, voting record, committee work, understanding district needs, name recognition, constituent services.

2. Personal characteristics: hardworking, young, old, personable, intelligent, energetic, ability to communicate, appearance, family life.

3. Issues/ideology/group ties: inflation, health insurance, welfare, government spending, taxes, energy, national defense, local issues, conservative, liberal, ties with and support from groups such as unions, business, farmers.

4. Party affiliation: Democrat, Republican, party ties, Democrat in Democratic district, Republican in Republican district.

5. Campaign organization: staff, money, volunteers, media, advertising, late start.

The direction of the responses was also recorded in the de-

---

*Intercoder reliability averaged 85 percent on the expanded coding scheme. Our five content themes do not grow out of any theory of human information processing. Lacking an elegant conceptual base, we have sim-

tailed coding scheme. For instance, the contestant might be perceived as stressing his or her own record or attacking the opponent's record. For this presentation, we do not preserve these distinctions but merely focus on the frequency of a named category.

On average, reporters supply as much detail about the campaigns of challengers as they do about those of incumbents, mentioning about five themes for each. This fact deserves highlighting, considering the evidence we report below about the disproportionate amount of coverage incumbents receive. Journalists learn a great deal about both political gladiators; they just write and publish more about one than the other.

An unkind critic can wonder why successful efforts to learn about challengers, yielding a bounty of information, should not produce a richer file of stories for public consumption.

The campaign as analyzed. We followed with a series of questions that shifted attention away from what the candidates were presenting and toward the reporters' interpretation of the campaigns. Our questions solicited judgments about the factors that would help or hinder contestants in their election bid: *Regardless of what the candidates are emphasizing, I'd like to ask what you feel are the strengths and weaknesses in their campaigns. What are (Candidate A's/B's) strengths? Any others? Weaknesses? Any others?*

Again journalists provided an abundance of descriptive material, offering an average of seven attributes for each contender. This material was coded according to the expanded and collapsed schemes used for the emphases, and is called *strengths* and *weaknesses* of the candidates.

The campaign as it appears in news articles. News articles were clipped for all papers in our sample, from September 27 through Election Day. We combed stories paragraph by paragraph. Wherever a candidate's name or reference appeared we noted the co-occurrence or absence of other information. This produced a content analysis of 5,183 paragraphs found in 731

---

ply imitated criteria for political reasoning proposed by other researchers interested in voter decision-making and campaign description (e.g., Kingdon 1966; Graber 1971; Russonello & Wolf 1979).

separate articles published in major daily newspapers covering 58 districts where incumbents faced a challenger.*

The substantive coding categories match those applied to the survey data. Examples for each of the thematic categories provide a flavor of the reportage available in congressional races:

1. Political attributes: "He has been what one Republican termed 'a model Congressman' in making frequent visits to the district and efficiently handling constituent requests." "He is at the pinnacle of a career distinguished by his chairmanship of a communications subcommittee."

2. Personal characteristics: "On the campaign trail, he likes to talk to the audience about 'where I'm coming from.' The Republican Congressman means, in part, that he sees himself as a product of his roots. He was born in 1942 in the little town of Onawa, Iowa, which is 60 miles from Omaha, Nebraska, and was the youngest of five children. His father was a construction crane operator. His mother was, and still is, a waitress." "Eventually she concluded 'there was nothing to fear' in Congress. 'I've almost been dead three times,' she said. 'I've become philosophical.' Those experiences include losing three children at birth and a trip to the intensive care unit after giving birth to her second child."

3. Issues/ideology/group ties: "Accusing his Democratic opponent of 'waffling' on the tax cut issue [the Republican congressional candidate] denounced President Carter's threat to veto pending tax cuts." "Two women's political organizations announced Tuesday that they are supporting fourteen women candidates for Congress, including. . . ." "She also received money this reporting period from TV producer [Norman] Lear . . . and he [the opponent] received $6,500 from the National Republican Congressional Committee and money from the National Rifle Association Victory Fund."

4. Party affiliation: "Republicans for years have found that running against Representative [Democratic incumbent] is like trying to hit an invisible target. . . . That's because the

---

*The total number of incumbent/challenger races in our sample is 71. Thirteen of these districts have major daily newspapers that failed to carry any pre-election coverage.

incumbent Democrat treats opponents like foreigners to whom he refuses to grant diplomatic recognition."

5. Campaign organization: "[X] has spent $23,924 during the last three months trying to hold on to the seat he won by a three-to-one margin last election." "While other Republican candidates struggle along on shoestring budgets and non-existent staffs, [X] has budgeted $40,000 and applied a fair measure of political sophistication in his quest." "A campaign aide commented that 'some things were beyond our control. We had a good drive, well-financed, and a lot of workers. But Governor [X] put a lot into theirs. We did a good job at registration, but the opposition did more than they ever had before.'"

Comparisons of content themes across the three views of campaigns reveal where the journalistic lens magnifies some components of political communication and where it dwarfs or bypasses others. Reporters' work results in a pool of relatively dispassionate information, compared with the self-serving advertising of the candidates. The electorate's capacity to reach reasoned judgments about candidates reflects, in part, the range and frequency of themes to which they are exposed. In tracing the translation processes from event to story, we offer explanations for the patterns that emerge and suggestions to remedy some of the journalistic defects that surface.

The View from Reporters

Emphases and strengths and weaknesses differ in striking and informative ways. And these journalistic perceptions depart from the copy appearing in daily newspapers.

When journalists speak of campaign emphases—how politicians are trying to sway voters—they almost always refer to two categories of information, which fall into the content themes we call issues/ideology/group ties and political attributes. Candidates are above all recognized for speaking out on particular policy positions—inflation, taxes, government spending, and a host of other national and local concerns. The average reporter noted that each contender emphasized between two and three different issues.

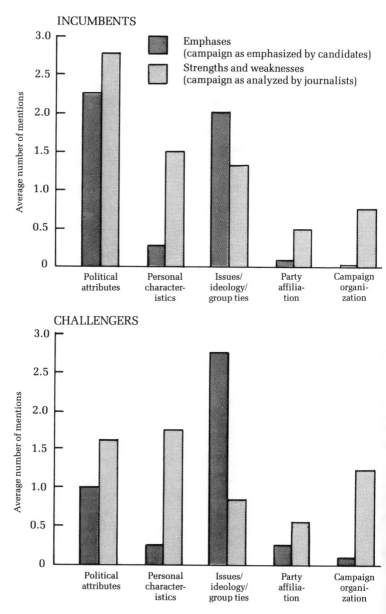

Fig. 1. Campaign as emphasized by candidates and as analyzed by journalists

Strikingly, issue-related topics recede when reporters turn to analyzing the strengths and weaknesses that they think will determine the election. This shift is particularly evident for challengers, where mentions of issues average fewer than one. Though reporters see challengers as emphasizing their positions on issues and their ties to groups in the district, they do not believe that this message carries much weight in affecting the vote. Instead, the success of challengers is thought to hinge on personal characteristics and political attributes.

The data in Figure 1 shed light on one cause of friction between politicians and reporters. We can pose the conflict as a simple question: which of the two groups knows the voter's mind better? Which correctly judges the electorate's "true" interest in issues? We lack conclusive evidence on this score, but tend to side with the politicians in their sense of what the voting public wants to know. Chapter Six provides some empirical support for our position. We argue for it on other grounds as well.

Candidates live in direct contact with their "market." We can expect them to be sensitive to nuances and claims that sway public support with highly rewarding or devastating personal consequences—election or defeat. Journalists, on the other hand, are insulated from public sentiment by their own bureaucracy and often by lack of media competition. Many studies have shown that reporters more often seek cues about their work from colleagues than from readers.

In singling out political attributes as the second major emphasis of congressional candidates, reporters speak mainly of experience in office and the assets and liabilities that accompany it. Political background is both heavily stressed and highly valued, especially for the incumbent. Journalists frequently cite committee work, past voting record, constituent services, name recognition, and familiarity with the legislative process. These are soft topics requiring simple newsgathering skills.

Personal characteristics represent another discrepancy between campaigns as emphasized by candidates and campaigns as analyzed by reporters. On the whole, candidates do not dwell on these characteristics in their appeals to voters. Yet journalists believe that they are very important factors in determining the outcome of a congressional race. These data are at odds with the conventional wisdom about contemporary politics. The belief that campaigners lean on personality and image and ignore issues is not confirmed by our reporters, who are, after all, paid observers of the local political scene.

There is a logic to why personal attributes loom so large in reporters' analyses of the campaigns. Some researchers have suggested that congressional elections are basically local phenomena, regardless of party identification, incumbency, and national sentiment. Mann (1978: 104), for example, notes that as "congressional campaigns become more and more divorced from local party organizations and more and more dependent upon the mass media, the likelihood increases that voters' decisions will turn on personal qualities of the candidates (real or alleged) that are not central to the job of the representative."

Reporters seem convinced that Mann is right. But we find it hard to see why issues cannot be locally oriented, too. The decline of party may have removed mechanisms for aggregating issues into an understandable mosaic or platform. This may account for the press's enthusiasm for analyzing candidates, especially challengers, in terms of personal characteristics.

Reporters more often cite campaign organization as a strength or weakness of a challenger than of an incumbent. Detailed coding (distinguishing strengths from weaknesses) reveals that most of these responses reflect perceived flaws in the campaign—not enough money, late start, small staff. If the level of campaign funding is any indication, fewer incumbents are afflicted with organizational liabilities than challengers (*Congressional Quarterly Weekly Report* 1979).

The fifth and final theme, party affiliation, is a minor part of the candidates' message to voters. It plays a comparatively limited role in reporters' evaluation of House races.

Newspaper Content

The sharp differences between emphases and strengths and weaknesses help clarify our understanding of the content themes appearing in news stories.* Evenhandedness in what reporters know and judge about incumbents and challengers is not matched by the actual press coverage each candidate receives. The most primitive measure—the number of name mentions a candidate receives—provides stunning evidence of the advantages of incumbency. In only 4 percent of the articles did incumbents' names fail to appear; the comparable figure for challengers is ten times greater, 40 percent.

What is the character of news copy associated with each contender, and how does this square with journalists' two views (emphases and strengths and weaknesses) of the campaigns? For incumbents, as Figure 2 shows, political attributes are overwhelmingly the focus of news coverage. Indeed, this type of information is most common in all views— candidates themselves emphasize it, reporters think it is highly influential in the success or failure of a campaign, and newspapers carry it. Fully 77 percent of the newspaper articles referring to incumbents included some mention of recent votes in the House, committee work, legislative experience, or the like. Liabilities linked with incumbency, such as an inability to keep staff or an abuse of the franking privilege, also crop up.†

*For most of this presentation of newspaper content, articles are the unit of study. This prevents the analysis of content themes from being distorted by reporting styles of the few papers that had sufficient newshole to run especially long stories about the election. Each article represents an opportunity for the reporter and the paper to command the reader's attention. We examine the proportion of articles that include at least one mention of the five themes of political information. Occasionally we present aggregate totals reflecting the prominence of content themes across all paragraphs in all articles. Chapter Four provides a detailed analysis of cumulative mentions.

†We cannot isolate campaign stories as such from articles referring to the daily activities of an incumbent as a member of the House. Even in the week just before the election, when journalistic attention is focused on campaign activities and less concerned with routine congressional duties, incumbents are mentioned in 88 percent of news articles, and challengers in only 52 percent.

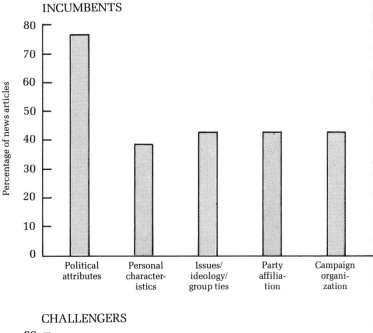

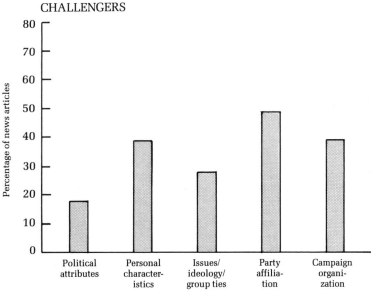

Fig. 2. Campaign as covered by newspapers

Incumbents receive fairly uniform coverage (38 percent to 43 percent of articles) in the other four categories of political information. Mentions of party appear frequently in print, more than one would expect from the candidates' emphases or from the reporters' judgments of the importance of party affiliation. This is due in large part to the coding scheme, which routinely recorded a party mention whenever the label Democrat or Republican was associated with a candidate's name.

The type of information printed about challengers contrasts vividly with that about incumbents. We have seen, for example, that political background is the second-most-important emphasis for challengers, and that reporters also cite this as an important strength or weakness for them. But this category of information rarely sees public print. Only 18 percent of the news stories on challengers deal with their political assets and liabilities, even though reporters see these themes as key criteria affecting electoral fortunes. An explanation is not hard to find. It is the lack of political background and past record in public office that reporters see as affecting a challenger's chances. This weakness cannot be converted easily into news copy that appears unprejudicial.

Challengers mount their voter appeals on issues, on their ties with political groups, and on ideological positions. Unfortunately for them, this political strategy falls on deaf ears in the journalistic community; reporters tend to assign little weight to this information as a genuine strength or weakness. And this reportorial judgment finds its ultimate expression in a lack of attention in news stories. Only 27 percent of articles link the challenger to an issue, group, or ideological stand.

Incumbents find easier access to newspaper readers for this category of information. Not only do reporters see these matters as of more importance for the incumbents' electoral success than for the challengers', but this translates into a substantially greater share of news stories on these topics (43 percent for incumbents against the challengers' 27 percent).

The absolute figures present an even more telling contrast. Over the entire campaign period, 1,161 paragraphs with issue content were published about incumbents, compared with 664 paragraphs, or slightly more than half as much, for challengers.

These results describe a frustrating journalistic maze facing challengers. Many lack experience in office and therefore cannot gain news attention by displaying evidence of the political skills demanded by the seat they seek. Challengers like to mount their campaigns on issues; but this strategy is discounted and frequently ignored by the press.

References to challengers' organizational prowess are even more prominent than the share of articles shown in Figure 2 suggests. When reporters refer to this topic—in 39 percent of articles—they usually write about it extensively. This swells the aggregate number of paragraphs to 892, making it the most prevalent type of information conveyed about challengers.

The remaining category of information, personal characteristics—age, speaking style, appearance, family, and the like—is considered important by many reporters, but this material must be excavated by journalistic initiative because it is rarely promoted by the candidates themselves. But we observe that though this is the least important subject of news stories for incumbents, it is one of the most important for challengers (39 percent of articles).

Issue Reporting and Candidates' Resources

Issue reporting by the media deserves additional attention for at least three reasons. First, attacks on the press for dwelling on personality to the exclusion of issues invite an empirical test. Second, candidates themselves are not of one mind about the degree to which success or failure at the polls hinges on the public awareness of issues. As Kingdon (1966) notes, winners in politics "congratulate" voters by attributing their success, in part, to the electorate's awareness of issues, whereas losers tend to "rationalize" their failure on the basis of their party affiliation. And third, recent work on voting behavior indicates a decline in party loyalty and increased focus on national issues, at least in presidential races. Nie, Verba, and Petrocik (1976) alert us to three factors necessary for issue voting: issues must be present and visible; they must affect voters' lives; and candidates must take differing stands. Research into media agenda-setting (Erbring, Goldenberg & Miller 1980; MacKuen in MacKuen & Coombs 1981) demonstrates that newspapers are implicated in at least the first two steps toward issue voting.

A better understanding of the treatment of issues in the press can be achieved by looking at the resources candidates bring to the campaign. We have suggested that the number of terms spent in office is the most important factor for incumbents, and that money is the most important for challengers.

Table 4 shows the median number of paragraph mentions about issue, ideological, and group-related topics for resource-poor and resource-rich incumbents and challengers. Though there is some variability, it is clear that the challenger who has money—and is perceived as a viable threat to the incumbent—gets coverage. The almost complete neglect of those challengers who do not run well-heeled campaigns is sobering.* With money challengers can do as well as or better than incumbents in gaining press coverage for their stands on issues; without it they face a hopeless situation.†

One explanation for differences between incumbent and challenger issue coverage argues that officeholders are supported by press aides, who know how to manage the media and how to get their employers' issue stands into news reports. In fact, part of our findings lead in this direction. In contested races, eight in ten incumbents had a press aide, compared with fewer than five in ten challengers. This im-

---

*We also examined the incumbent-challenger/high-low resource differences for each of the other four categories of political information. We found the same pattern: above-average expenditures by the challenger make a difference in the number of paragraph mentions; the years in office do not make a difference for incumbents.

†When incumbent resources are defined by total FEC expenditures, we find that the high-resource group receives more press attention in all content themes than the low-resource group. We chose not to present incumbent resources in this way because an increase in competition depends largely on the efforts of challengers. As Jacobson (1978: 469) notes, "The more incumbents spend, the worse they do; the reason is that they raise and spend money in direct proportion to the magnitude of the electoral threat posed by the challenger, but this reactive spending fails to offset the progress made by the challenger that inspires it in the first place."

TABLE 4

Median Number of Paragraph Mentions About
Issues/Ideology/Group Ties, by
Candidacy and Resources

Group covered	No. of mentions	Group covered	No. of mentions
Incumbents		Challengers	
Low resources	11	Low resources	1
High resources	6	High resources	9

NOTE: For the definition of low and high resources, see pp. 30–31.

balance in human resources might not account for much of
the difference in issue coverage, though, if research by Kaid
(1976) and Vermeer (1978) is pertinent. In separate studies of
news releases, they found that these more frequently involved the announcement of campaign events and personal
information than the candidate's stands on issues.

Discussion

This chapter highlights weaknesses and the imbalance in
press coverage of congressional campaigns. Though the results are understandable, they should not be taken for granted.
The first order of business by the press is to deliver news—
usually defined as what happened yesterday on the campaign trail. Issues may slip from view because candidates
often have nothing new to say about them. Contenders for
elected office are equipped with a standard speech they make
before various audiences throughout the campaign. Reporters who follow them to these appearances also receive daily
news releases and are literally swamped with redundant information. We should understand why journalists look for
something that would indicate a change or contradiction instead of repetition; all else failing, they can report on the way
the candidate looks, dresses, and speaks.

The incumbents' advantage in issue coverage is a natural
consequence of officeholding. Legislative work is news; campaign speeches and releases referring to bills that affect the
district are news. Whether the incumbent is officially cam-

paigning or engaging in ordinary congressional matters, there is copy to be mined. The challenger does not enjoy this pragmatic edge. Promises, proposals, and vows of future legislative action are not seen as newsworthy.

Finally, personal traits are the stuff of human-interest material, the kind of story assignment on which many journalists cut their teeth.

Journalistic avoidance of issue-oriented subjects has several implications for political communication. This lack of reporting takes place against a backdrop of declining party identification among voters and structurally weakened parties that are often hard put to recruit candidates and finance their run for office. Traditionally, the label "Democrat" forecast support for full employment and resistance to sharply increased defense budgets; "Republican" signaled support for policies that aided the business community. As the importance of party identification fades, voters lose ready cues about a candidate's point of view. Citizens abandon traditional anchor points for their own political beliefs.

Given declining party discipline among officeholders and declining party fealty among the electorate, voters—if they are to cast ballots in ways that maximize their interests—need information that can replace traditional cues. News accounts that include the candidates' stands on issues, group affiliations, and ideological leanings could offer valuable assistance. Where these themes are overlooked in reporting, a major prop is removed from policy coordination between Congress and the federal executive. This can only encourage candidates to personalize their political strategy.

Reportorial inattention to challengers' views about issues may have become a self-fulfilling prophecy in which neglect probably breeds public indifference. The routine reelection of incumbents, with increasingly lopsided vote margins, may be one outcome.

Perhaps these journalistic habits help explain the observation that Congress is doing more but accomplishing less in terms of enacted legislation (Allen Schick, speech to the American Political Science Association Congressional Fellows, quoted in Mann 1978: 105).

The disadvantages that confront challengers are more acute than limited name recognition and inattention by the press. The only category of information in which challengers enjoy parity with incumbents is personal characteristics. Naturally, such information is often freighted with political significance, and one might argue that personal repute and family offer useful guides for the voters. But personal characteristics rarely predict a candidate's vote on legislation that determines the taxes people pay or the social services they receive, or that authorizes a military adventure. News stories about policy and group ties may be dry and burdensome to report, difficult to dramatize or sprinkle with human interest. But hints about issue preferences would help attentive voters identify reasons for accepting or rejecting newcomers to the political scene.

The present mix of language in written news reports, giving incumbents the edge on both political background and issues, imposes hopeless odds on challengers. Hence, their only avenue to the House is to demonstrate that they are superior to the incumbent in personality or character. In our view, these practices in political journalism limit the scope of rational voter choice.

IV

News Coverage and Electoral Competition

COMPETITION for seats in the U.S. House of Representatives has declined so seriously in the last 15 years that even in the Watergate-tainted elections of 1974, 88 percent of the incumbents who ran were reelected. And furthermore, their margin of victory has increased significantly. If, as Asher and Weisberg (1978) contend, policy change in Congress results more from the replacement of incumbents than from shifts in the voting behavior of those who remain in office, movement in new policy directions would turn on retirement, death, and the rare defeat of an incumbent, rather than on biennial elections. But it is the electoral process, theoretically, by which officials are held accountable. The incumbents' need to defend their record and renew their right to return to Washington presumably guarantees a correspondence between their decisions and the citizens' preferences. Weakened electoral competition, our results show, derives in part from press performance, a previously neglected element on the congressional campaign scene.

We begin with the premise that balanced journalistic coverage is a point of reference in gauging the health of electoral processes. Comparisons between types of electoral situations and how closely each comes to balanced coverage suggest problems in press performance.* Our look at newspapers as

---

*We distinguish balance from bias. Bias presumes the distortion of events. Balance can be measured in terms of space or time devoted to one

vehicles for helping citizens make informed decisions ignores partisan campaigning for the moment.

This chapter looks at the information appearing in news columns during the five weeks prior to the general election— for each contender and by competitiveness of vote outcome. Specifically, we find:

1. News attention, for both incumbents and challengers, varies directly with the competitiveness of the race; tight races receive vastly more coverage than less hotly contested races.

2. Incumbents draw much more coverage than challengers in tight races.

3. This large discrepancy in coverage cannot be explained by reporters' effort: journalists exert the same amount of energy covering both candidates.

4. This discrepancy can be best understood by examining *types* of reporting themes; some news topics are treated in a balanced way, others are not.

5. An important imbalance stems from the high priority newspapers assign to political experience. It is this news judgment that does the most to focus attention on officeholders and to keep challengers in the background.

These are the highlights. We move from results to explanation, suggesting reasons why equal reportorial work pays disparate dividends. It is a disturbing story that both confirms other analyses of House elections and offers new insight into press habits.

The Current Context of Congressional Races

The tendency for House members to coast to reelection has become even more marked since the 1970's. Not only has the win-loss record of sitting House members managed to float at or above the 90 percent mark, but their victories have become increasingly lopsided. The increasing ease with which

---

person or another. In this analysis, balanced coverage means that certain content themes appear with equal frequency over the campaign period. Importantly, bias cannot be inferred from imbalance. (For a discussion of these issues, see Comstock 1980: 50–56.)

House members manage to garner constituent support is vividly displayed by Mayhew (1974). Data from 1956 through 1972 illustrate that increasingly fewer districts fall in the competitive range (i.e., 45–55 percent) and more are in the area that is safe for incumbents.*

This trend describes only reelection bids to the House of Representatives. Open races have more competitive outcomes; as noted earlier, in our 1978 sample, on average, incumbent/challenger races were won by a margin of 36 percent, compared with 24 percent for the open contests. This pattern does not characterize bids for Senate seats, which are less secure than those in the lower chamber.

The 1980 elections saw the defeat of some well-known and important incumbents: in the Senate, George McGovern, Frank Church, Birch Bayh, and John Culver; in the House, John Brademas and Lionel Van Deerlin, among others. The fall of these giants should not be read as a departure from the norm, however. In the House, 92 percent of those seeking reelection were returned for another two-year stint.

Before the number of competitive districts plummeted, an incumbency effect was anticipated, at least indirectly. Stokes and Miller (1966) noted that incumbents were more frequently recognized by their constituents, and that voters were more likely to support a candidate whose name they knew. This leads to the inference that increased visibility confers electoral advantage.

Incumbency advantages form a backdrop to the present analysis of press performance. Explanations that political scientists offer for rates of reelection have largely ignored media variables (a recent exception is M. Robinson 1981). Their accounts can be grouped into three camps: (1) incumbent-centered reasons, (2) voter-centered changes, and (3) changes in congressional functions. Let us look briefly at each explanation.

---

*But even so, members of Congress fear defeat, with some justification. At least one in three eventually is tossed out of office by voters (Erikson 1978). Almost half won their seat in the first place by taking it away from the opposite party; a reflective incumbent might easily imagine history repeating itself.

Incumbent-centered reasons. We can quickly dismiss the argument of Tufte (1973) that competitive districts have vanished due to the incumbents' ability to control redistricting. Ferejohn (1977) demonstrates that the House members' edge appears both in districts that have been redrawn and in those that have not.

Mayhew (1974; 1976) asserts that much of what the incumbent does is focused on getting reelected. He cites a number of strategies toward this end: advertising (keeping the member's name before the home folks), credit-taking (convincing constituents that the member is responsible for desirable government decisions), position-taking (roll-call votes from which the member gains benefits by taking the "correct" stand, independent of policy impact), and capitalizing on the perquisites of office (travel allocations, staff, and mail).[*]

With these resources, House members can continue to make their presence felt.[†] Representatives may be advertising themselves better: for instance, the number of pieces of mail sent from the Capitol peaks in even years, and especially in the months just prior to a general election. The advantage could be remarkably simple; the "more hundreds of thousands of messages congressmen rain down on constituents, the more votes they get" (Mayhew 1974: 311).

Recent data underscore the contention that federally financed computers, franking privileges, and public funds for direct-mail experts have given an edge to members of Congress seeking reelection. It is difficult to estimate the size of this subsidy, but available records suggest that "computer time, labor, paper, and the franking privilege may add up to $100 million every election year" (Burnham 1980: 96). And these efforts are increasingly used in reelection bids. Though the number of letters mailed by House members in response to specific inquiries has remained fairly stable

---

[*]Cover & Brumberg (1982) inspected one of these incumbency advantages closely. The franking privilege allows representatives to deluge voters with government pamphlets and other materials. These boost the incumbent's name recognition and create positive evaluations. Challengers make far less use of the mails and do so, of course, at their own expense.

[†]In Mayhew's view, incumbents have also benefited from the erosion of party loyalty.

(about 2,000,000 a year), the growing availability of computer services has made it possible for mass mailings to increase just before election day. House members dispatched some 31,000,000 pieces of mail in September 1974, 35,000,000 in September 1976, and 40,000,000 in September 1978.*

Many feel that the frank and computer technology are destroying the elective and legislative process. Representative Patricia Schroeder of Colorado is highly critical:

The use of computerized mailing lists, heavily subsidized by the public, has caused substantial changes in the quality of Congress. It is outrageous. It is an incumbent's dream. It has enabled all Congressmen to write their constituents and tell them exactly what they want to hear. The frank and the technology together have turned most congressional offices into full-time public-relations firms rather than offices that spend at least part of each day thinking seriously about serious issues (quoted in Burnham 1980: 98).

Voter-centered changes. The voter-centered explanation of the incumbency effect has a number of disciples (e.g., Burnham 1975; Ferejohn 1977; Cover 1977). They emphasize changes in mass-voting behavior, independent of the candidates' efforts at self-promotion.

One trend is clear: voters show loosening ties to traditional political cues (party). More people are refusing to vote a straight ticket, and party defections fall heavily into a pro-incumbent pattern. Where in 1958 just over half of all votes cast across party lines went to the incumbent, the figure has gradually edged upward, to stand at about three-quarters in the 1970's (Cover & Mayhew 1977). This represents an important shift in electoral behavior.

Some suggest the pattern of crossover voting is due, in part, to the familiarity that accrues to House members. Current officeholders are well known and well liked (Mann & Wolfinger 1980); challengers in these elections suffer from low visibility, and few voters display much feeling about them.† In fact, party defections would be less loaded toward

---

*A congressional rule currently prohibits mass mailings 60 days before a primary or general election.

†But incumbents do not have an advantage in name recall; voters' ability to recall has not increased. This suggests that researchers have been using a

incumbents if more challengers could make themselves favorably known to voters.

Changes in congressional functions. The third approach shares some features of the other two. It contends that voters correctly perceive that reelecting an incumbent benefits the district. Great Society legislation has created large sums of money to be distributed to districts, bringing an increasingly complex government bureaucracy (Fiorina 1977a; 1977b). Voters recognize that a House member takes care of "sticky" snarls in paperwork and captures a fair share of the federal largesse for the home district. Attention to these tasks crowds out programmatic and controversial duties. Dispensing money, providing constituent services, and the like are nonpartisan, yet pay a handsome electoral dividend. The most important asset for performing these functions is experience in office, knowing the ropes. The longer a person has been in Washington, the better equipped he or she is to handle effectively and efficiently the routine demands of the job.

But this explanation is vulnerable because these duties have been a feature of congressional life since the late 1950's, well before competitive districts "vanished" from the political landscape. As Clapp (1963: 50) observed:

The significant increase in the impact of government on the daily lives of the population that has characterized the period since the early 1930's has thrust increasing responsibilities on members of the Congress. Bewildered, sometimes engulfed, by their new relationship with government, citizens have turned to their representatives in Washington for assistance. One result has been the steady rise in the time which legislators allocate to performance of the "representative" function, at the expense of activities commonly associated with the "legislative" role.

With these three explanations as a backdrop, we examine the press treatment afforded incumbents and challengers.

---

poor measure of awareness. "Recall" has generally been measured by the question: "Do you happen to remember the names of the candidates for Congress who ran in this district last November?" Many voters who cannot recall candidates' names can nonetheless recognize a name when it is presented to them, a situation analogous to the voting booth. (See Mann 1978; Tedin & Murray 1979; Mann & Wolfinger 1980.)

Though these views do not implicate the press explicitly, its performance can be woven into each.

The incumbent-centered explanation relies on the notion that current officeholders command assets that can be exploited to win electoral support. An unnoticed, or at least unmentioned, resource is access to the press. The incumbent, being of official status, is more newsworthy than the challenger, even in the final days of a hotly contested campaign. Preferential press coverage in local newspapers is another incumbent perquisite.

The second explanation posits a substantial shift in the voting behavior of the electorate. Traditional cues (i.e., party ties) have deteriorated, and been replaced with a new one—incumbency. House members have an easier time obtaining journalistic attention, and the information conveyed about them squares well with what voters feel is important in a representative. The press is a handmaiden to the interests of the current officeholder, relaying precisely the type of information (experience in office) on which many voters base their choice.

The third explanation emphasizes the incumbent's edge in knowing the ropes and securing benefits for the district. Our study shows newspapers reporting the kind of information that underscores this activity.

The evidence we marshal does not rule out any of these explanations; all of them receive some support. We discover how press habits and routines contribute to several electoral advantages House members have acquired—in ways that have been overlooked by others.

Coverage and Competition

Candidates acknowledge the role of newspapers in their bid for office. But they do not feel that editorial endorsements are the only, or even the most significant, type of support a newspaper can provide. As one of Kingdon's (1966) informants noted, "I had most of them [endorsements]. But the editorial backing does not help unless they give you a story every day and push it. Five per cent of the readers read the editorial page. And when it comes out two or three days before the election, it doesn't help much" (p. 51). Unsuccessful candidates have been quick to point out that they were unable to obtain coverage in news columns (Kingdon 1966; Fishel 1973).

The phenomenon is hardly new. Kelley (1959), analyzing press coverage in two competitive congressional districts, found a preferential news treatment of House members, and was forced to conclude that "incumbency and at least tacit support by the paper were key factors in a congressional candidate's gaining an advantage in news coverage" (p. 448).

The more competitive the race, the more newsworthy it is. Our 1978 data show that coverage of incumbents and challengers varies directly with the closeness of the race. Visibility of candidates in news columns plunges as the comparisons shift from close races to lopsided contests.

Figure 3 shows the median number of name mentions for incumbents and challengers in 1978. Three types of elections are contrasted: 14 tight races, in which losers got at least 42 percent of the vote; 30 medium races, in which losers got at least 30–41 percent; and 27 lopsided races, in which losers got less than 30 percent.

Press performance in the tight races is of special interest to us for obvious reasons; these are contests where new blood might enter political circulation. As the figure shows, even here incumbents, with a median of 110 name mentions, outscore their opponents by 30 mentions or more. This stands as a substantial lead in public attention.*

In the less competitive contests, by comparison, incumbents and challengers receive more balanced coverage, at least in absolute terms. In the medium races, each draws 30 to 40 mentions. In the lopsided elections, little newshole is granted to either congressional contender, each receiving about six mentions.

The incumbents' absolute lead in tight races merits special

---

*These absolute levels of news attention underestimate press coverage because of omissions by the clipping service. We returned to a sample of microfilm records of newspaper files, searching for evidence that these omissions introduced a systematic bias. This additional search confirmed the relationships between news play, type of candidacy, and competitiveness.

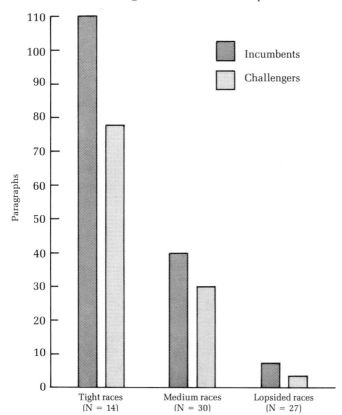

Fig. 3. Median number of paragraph mentions, by competitiveness of race

attention. These are the contests with well-funded challengers who purchase advertising, arrange speeches, and mount
newsworthy events. The press is out in full force. The public's interest is piqued, to the degree that voters ever pay
heed to congressional contests. With an audience at hand,
any disparity in journalistic effort is bound to have political
effects. Where serious campaigns are being waged, gaps in
coverage probably signal substantial problems in the press's
treatment of politics.

Favored journalistic practice in the medium and lopsided
races is less consequential—even where it may be propor-
tionately the same as tight contests. Incumbents enjoy an ad-

vantage of a few name mentions (no more than 10), often the result of only a story or two—a difference that would probably pass unnoticed, except by participants and the most avid voters.

The Incumbency Effect in News Coverage

The 14 most competitive races present opportunities for political turnover, and further analysis of them can throw the priorities and mechanisms of press behavior into stark relief.* We find that the incumbents' advantage in news play is not due to a disparity in journalistic effort: reporters' activity scores in covering incumbents and challengers are exactly the same.†

But an important difference emerges when we examine the link between journalistic effort and its outcome. "Units" of journalistic effort—interviewing, attending press conferences, quizzing groups, and more—convert directly into news play when reporters are covering incumbents. The correlation between activity and name mentions is .82, highly significant with only 14 elections to analyze. The same is not true in the coverage of challengers, where the correlation reaches only .42, not statistically significant.

What is it about incumbents, compared with challengers, that allows journalistic effort to translate into such whoppingly large numbers of mentions? Details about why challengers' campaign stories fail to reach the newspaper reader can be gleaned by looking closely at specific content themes found in news articles. Table 5 helps tell the story. It illustrates the crippling liability challengers face with the press—even where they succeed in attracting electoral support.

---

*To reassure ourselves that results from these 14 districts were not the product of some quirk in sampling, the competitive races were analyzed on a number of standard criteria. Encouragingly, the districts span geographically from north to south and east to west and include newspapers with daily circulations ranging from 20,000 to more than 1,000,000. These races are characterized by high expenditures. Eleven of the incumbents and 13 of the challengers spent above-average amounts.

†The degree of journalistic effort put into campaign coverage does vary directly with the competitiveness of the race. But at each level of competitiveness, newspeople work as hard on current officeholders as on their opposition.

TABLE 5
*Median Number of Paragraph Mentions About
Content Themes in 14 Tight Races*

Theme	Coverage of incumbents	Coverage of challengers
Political attributes	49	4
Issues/ideology/group ties	29	12
Campaign organization	22	27
Personal characteristics	10	13

News copy about incumbents leans heavily on political attributes—such as experience in office, name recognition, and constituent services. House members also manage to draw coverage of their issue stands and affiliation with electorally significant groups. References to challengers' organizational prowess or liabilities—contributors, staff, registration drives, and the like—command most of their journalistic ink.

Candidates receive equivalent news play in two categories, i.e., personal characteristics and campaign organization. But news treatment is widely in favor of the incumbent on issues and even more so on political attributes. In the following pages we discuss in more detail the journalistic coverage of each content theme.

Coverage of political attributes. The largest discrepancy in contenders' coverage is in the political-attributes category; incumbents receive 12 times as many mentions as challengers. Some preferential treatment comes as no surprise, in light of the advantages of officeholding we have discussed, but the sheer magnitude of the discrepancy provokes further analysis.

Journalistic effort cannot explain the disparity in political coverage. The relationship between work and number of mentions with political themes is very strong, *and similar*, for both contenders: .78 for incumbents and .71 for challengers. So the newsgathering process is similar for each contender, but yields dissimilar results.

Reporters work hard, but fail to find much to write about on the political background of challengers. Why? The answer is probably simple, if depressing: challengers usually do not have the raw material—past experience in office, legislative skills, constituent services. House members, on the other hand, have an almost endless reservoir to tap.

Incumbents, in *all* electoral situations, outdistance challengers in the amount of news copy referring to political qualifications and experience. This need not necessarily impose hopeless obstacles against challengers, but in fact it usually does. First, political information is important to voters in choosing a candidate because of new congressional functions. Second, there is no substitution effect; journalists do not direct readers' attention to challengers' stands on issues as a substitute for missing political background.

Experience is the quality journalists value most in congressional candidates, as our findings in Chapter Three suggest. Voters seem to agree. An early study (Leuthold 1968) of ten California elections found that voters looked first for signs of a candidate's qualifications for the duties of office. Because a term or more in the House is the best indicator of this ability, incumbents are likely to hold a distinct advantage over challengers.

More than half of all the advertising appeals in Leuthold's study were based on "qualities of the candidate." But within this category incumbents presented less personal and more political information because they had a public service record to promote. Seniority was always emphasized, regardless of the length of time served.

Unfortunately, challengers in too many instances have little political background and expertise to tout. Though the recent literature on recruitment is spotty (see Snowiss 1966; Fiellin 1967; Olson 1978), the consensus is that "political parties and their leadership permit the self-recruitment of poorly prepared, unexperienced, and naïve candidates" (Huckshorn & Spencer 1971: 43). More recent analyses concur: House incumbents benefit from the scarcity of serious challenge as well as from the resources of the office (Mann & Wolfinger 1980).*

---

* The considerations that lead people to challenge incumbents lie beyond our analysis. Jacobson (1980; 1981; Jacobson & Kernell 1981) has pointed to

We favor the following account for why incumbency draws preferential press attention. Unlike Fiorina, we cannot argue that the conditions affecting press-candidate relationships have altered during the past 20 years; our study may have captured evidence of media habits that have endured a long time.

Let us accept the thesis that House members' duties have changed as a result of the great waves of domestic legislation that have been passed (Fiorina 1977a; 1977b). Theoretically, members can spend their time doing three things: (1) taking issue positions, (2) bringing home the bacon, and (3) providing constituent services. The expansion of the federal bureaucracy (in part underwritten and promoted by Congress) into welfare and medical services, consumer affairs, environmental protection, education programs, and the like has altered demands on House members. Specifically, they must devote most of their time and attention to noncontroversial, issue-barren tasks; "unsticking" services—clearing overdue payments to a Vietnam veteran, expediting Social Security checks, helping to obtain a federal grant for housing or law enforcement, looking into a passport request—are the stuff of a representative's days. The more members tend to constituent needs and seek cash for home districts, the less time they have for crafting laws. Pork-barrel projects and constituent services attract bipartisan support. But issue stands are divisive; with every vote cast or policy position asserted, representatives please some members of the electorate and displease others.

House members have always been concerned that their districts get a fair share of the available "goods"; and they have always attended to constituent requests. But with the growth of federal programs, there are more goods to be distributed, and consequently more need for an energetic and concerned contact in Washington. Experience "in Washing-

---

candidates' experience in lower office and political circumstances that encourage able people to make a bid for Congress. Some candidates run and make a puzzling use of media, including broadcast spots, for more covert reasons; they expect the campaign to benefit their law practice, real estate business, or other enterprise.

ton and congressional seniority count when dealing with the bureaucracy. . . . The incumbency effect is not only understandable, it is rational. And it would grow over time as increasing numbers of citizens come to regard their Congressman as a troubleshooter in Washington bureaucracies" (Fiorina 1977a: 180). Constituents have come to appreciate tenure in office; one result is increasingly large vote margins on election day.

What does the growth in bureaucracy have to do with news reporting? Lots. On the campaign trail, incumbents emphasize their familiarity with Washington, their prompt constituent services, their success in securing federal grants, and their understanding of the district's needs—in short, their record of service. As we have seen, journalists recognize these campaign emphases and acknowledge their importance in the election results. These topics reflect (1) what House members do with their time, (2) what reporters perceive as important, and (3) what, in part, voters look for in choosing their candidates.* Hence, it comes as no surprise that political experience and performance are the most prevalent themes in campaign reporting.

Incumbents do nonlegislative work that is subsequently promoted on the campaign trail and carried in local newspapers. There is no way that challengers can compete on these grounds.

---

*Mann and Wolfinger (1980) analyzed responses to a battery of questions on citizen-initiated contact with representatives. The items were as follows: *Have you (or anyone in your family living here) ever contacted Representative (name) or anyone in (his/her) office?*; *Was the contact . . . to express an opinion, to seek information, to seek help on a problem?*; *Did you get a response from your Representative or (his/her) office?*; *How satisfied were you with the response?*; *Do you know anyone else who has contacted Representative (name) or anyone else in (his/her) office?*; *Did this (person/group) get a response?*; and *If you had (another/a) problem that Representative (name) could do something about, do you think (he/she) would be helpful?* The authors find that responding to constituent requests "paid no special vote dividend for House members" (p. 268). But corroborating both Fiorina's argument and the data presented here, they concede that "a reputation for service may have been more valuable. . . . It is likely that Congressmen build a reputation for service in a variety of ways, exploiting vehicles for mass publicity without limiting themselves to direct servicing of constituent requests" (*ibid.*).

Coverage of issues. It is widely believed that the positions taken by candidates for Congress have little impact on the voters' choices (see Stokes & Miller 1966; Mann 1978; Mann & Wolfinger 1980). The public is seen as largely unaware of where the contestants stand. Voters' open-end evaluations of contenders are "thin and highly personalized, with little apparent ideological or issue content" (Mann & Wolfinger 1980: 631). Many candidates expect their policy record to be relatively unimportant in their races (Mann 1978).

Yet our infatuation with fuller coverage of issue appeals persists, for at least three reasons. First, we present evidence in Chapter Six that issues are more important to voters than commonly thought. Second, a basic assumption of any theory of representative democracy is that there is a link between elections and policymaking. This makes the argument for issue coverage particularly persuasive in view of the plunge in electoral participation in recent years. In 1978, only 35 percent of the eligible voters, a select corner of the electorate with more than average education and political interest, cast ballots for the U.S. House. It is reasonable to expect campaigns and news copy to include substantive nourishment. Third, challengers, crippled by lack of tenure, are not able to attract news attention by exhibiting what they have done in office. Parity in the coverage of policy positions represents one way to right the imbalance. Contenders can develop platforms on local, national, and international matters, and these stands can be unearthed by journalists.

Still, it turns out that even when issues are reported, incumbents get preferential treatment. Incumbents get 29 issue mentions to their opponents' 12.

There is more to this story. Candidates differ in the extent to which they discuss issues on the campaign trail. Some avoid, ignore, or dismiss them; others concentrate on them (see Table 6). Issue for issue, incumbents manage to attract more news attention than challengers. High-emphasis challengers almost attain the news play afforded incumbents. Curiously, low-emphasis incumbents still come by considerable coverage, but low-emphasis challengers barely make a dent.

TABLE 6

Median Number of Paragraph Mentions About
Issues/Ideology/Group Ties
in 14 Tight Races

Group covered	No. of mentions	Group covered	No. of mentions
Incumbents		Challengers	
Low emphasis	21	Low emphasis	9
High emphasis	42	High emphasis	36

NOTE: Candidates' emphases, as perceived by reporters, were dichotomized for this analysis: low emphasis means no issue or only one was emphasized; high emphasis means two or more issues were emphasized.

Why do incumbents gain considerable coverage on issues, even when they do not speak to them? The answer is that political attributes have a sort of tandem effect: when political service is mentioned, issues are likely to be mentioned too. As we have seen, incumbents sweep through the campaign period drawing lots of copy on their Washington duties. Even for those who do not stress programmatic matters, the correlation between issue content and political content is very high (rho = .95). Incumbents have political credentials. House members are newsworthy, and their official status validates the coverage of their stands on the issues, regardless of what they choose to emphasize in their campaign.

This is not the case for challengers. They cannot compensate with issues for their inability to point to their services to the voters. It would be encouraging to find meager amounts of political copy supplemented by impressive issue coverage. This does not occur. In the 14 tight races, only one challenger received this type of news treatment. Promises from a contender without a political record lack news value.*

* A fact that is not missed by those who lose out in news coverage and in votes. As Huckshorn and Spencer found (1971: 225), "The gap between what a campaign was and what it should be caused much anguish and self-criticism among losers. They pled for policy debates and were forced into personal recriminations. They spoke against the incumbent's record and were met by silence. They wanted to exploit important social and economic questions but ended by emphasizing niggling and unimportant ones."

The story is simple, if disappointing. Competitive elections provide unrealized opportunities for balanced journalistic performance. Reporters play incumbents more intensively in the news, with two major consequences: (1) challengers have difficulty communicating their stands on the issues to newspaper readers; and (2) challengers cannot get "substitute" coverage for slim political credentials by emphasizing their stands. Hence challengers' names appear much less frequently during the general campaign period.

Coverage of campaign organization. For challengers, references to campaign organization are the most newsworthy angle of their bid for office. They get slightly more news mentions on this theme (27) than their opponents (22).

One might argue that spending patterns, budget allocations, contributors, and the like are important stories. A candidate's ability to raise money, to supervise personnel, to buy media in sensible and cost-effective ways, may represent a repertoire of managerial skills analogous to those required for congressional duties. Smart tactics and sound electioneering may translate into more money and goods for the home district.

If this were the case, we would expect reporters to substitute organizational references for challengers' absent or negligible experience in government. Unfortunately, we found no such substitution. In the 14 tight races, there were only two cases where reporters pried deeply into organizational matters when they could not mine much copy about the challenger's political background.

One explanation travels the following course: challengers who mount a viable campaign come by coverage because this engages a proven news peg—the incumbent. An officeholder who might lose in the general election is news. We cannot test this directly, but we marshal some presumptive evidence in support.

First, journalistic effort on incumbent campaigns converts directly into coverage of the campaign organization (the correlation between work and copy is .60). By contrast, challengers draw this kind of coverage without much reportorial exertion (rho = .21). Second, though we cannot retrace footsteps or reconstruct events with absolute precision, we suspect that the story starts with the newsworthy official (the incumbent) who is spending, planning, staffing, and organizing. Word of a threat, a strong challenger, has to be documented. It is difficult for a reporter to craft a news article about the possible tumble of a sitting representative without mentioning the opponent. Sure enough, when stories about fund-raising drives, volunteers, and contributors appear about one candidate, they appear about the other (rho = .72). And, importantly, this balancing act can be achieved with little journalistic effort: a phone call or two, or a peek at the latest FEC forms.

The point is worth emphasizing: a serious, well-funded campaign by a challenger does not guarantee journalistic attention. The incumbent is the necessary condition, the news peg. The amount of money raised by a challenger is not newsworthy as such, but a head-to-head comparison is.

Coverage of personal characteristics. This category of information draws balanced news treatment in absolute terms, but not in relative terms: a larger share of the challenger's mentions are of a personal nature. Relationships between effort and copy are moderate and similar for each. Culling through the newspaper clippings alerts us to a common journalistic technique—the biographical profile. This sort of coverage probably occurs because personal stories are easy to produce and easy to balance. Both candidates have an age, a marital status, children or no children, a certain educational level, a previous occupation, a polished or poor speaking style. These stories do not make tremendous demands on a reporter's time; and background information is often readily available in political almanacs and the candidates' own press packages.

Discussion

The context within which House elections take place has changed dramatically over the last 20 years. The declining importance of parties, intervention by PACs, increased campaign costs, sophisticated media strategies, and a stability in House membership are among these new developments.

This chapter casts light on another feature of the political landscape: journalistic performance.

Throughout, we have contended that news columns are the most important nonpartisan tool for assisting voters in choosing candidates. This, of course, represents a familiar view of the press: its function as the fourth branch of government, with an obligation to inform the public as fully as possible. This implies that candidates, regardless of party affiliation or other status, will be covered thoroughly.

Of course, one would not expect coverage of the two contenders to balance out each day. We are aware that there is considerable variation among campaigns. For instance, candidates who do not face opposition in a primary may be late off the blocks in raising money, organizing resources, and gaining attention. But the finding we highlight—the preferential treatment afforded incumbents—occurs throughout the election period. Even during the last week of the campaign, well after Congress has adjourned and when candidates are at the peak of electioneering, newspapers continue to play incumbents more prominently than their opponents. In the most competitive contests, incumbents were mentioned in 92 percent of the news stories we studied, compared with 78 percent for challengers. In the most lopsided races, the challengers' visibility sank even lower; they were mentioned in less than half the stories (48 percent), whereas incumbents were mentioned in every one.

This analysis of press performance confirms the incumbency advantage; any account of communication and political behavior must grapple with it. We go beyond familiar observations dealing with the resources incumbents command, weakening party identification among the electorate, and gratitude for pork-barrel and errand-running duties.*

*It is interesting to note that intellectual blinders have imposed a narrow view of which discipline is appropriate for one kind of research and which appropriate for another. Why has the nonpartisan press not been subjected to closer scrutiny? Political scientists believe that media coverage affects voters, but there is a widespread assumption that this coverage is the result of candidate behavior. Hence, the focus has been on "controlled" media, namely advertising. Campaigns have been dissected by the amount of money spent, the type of medium used, and the messages emphasized. Few

Incumbents enjoy special access to the press. Reporters tune coverage to the governmental experience candidates bring to contests. Political background is the characteristic communicated most in news stories. Challengers lacking lengthy records of public service enter the electoral arena shorn of cues for news stories.

We have paid special attention to the tightest House races. There, incumbents (usually faced by well-financed and serious challengers) outscore their opponents in news play by a wide margin. Much of this gap is due to greater journalistic attention to the incumbents' political qualifications than to those of their competitors.

There is a deeper significance to these results. The correlation between political themes and the other categories of information about the candidates is massive. If candidates fail to attract news attention for lack of political background, they will fail to win news play on other counts as well. Reporters do not substitute coverage of issues, which challengers often stress, for this material.

Students of congressional elections (e.g., Hinckley 1980a, 1980b; Mann & Wolfinger 1980) have suggested that researchers should shift their attention away from incumbents and what they do right, to challengers and the conditions hindering and facilitating their election. We have discovered a major obstacle for challengers in their bid for office: they are severely handicapped by low visibility. In voter analyses, Hinckley (1980a) finds candidates in open races do not differ appreciably from incumbents on evaluative ratings. Challengers of incumbents are the ones who suffer relative anonymity.

Of course, current officeholders have had two years or more to communicate their names and messages of performance and promise. And of course incumbents, being of official status, are simply more newsworthy than their oppo-

---

studies have focused on "uncontrolled" media: endorsements and news columns. A recent exception (Coombs, in MacKuen & Coombs 1981) found that newspaper editorials have a significant impact in Senate and gubernatorial races. Our research suggests that the strict distinction between controlled and uncontrolled media is less accurate than previously acknowledged. Incumbents control resources by which they gain column inches and name mentions.

nents. Furthermore, the preferential coverage of incumbents and lopsided editorial endorsements may be motivated by well-intended and sound decisions.

Yet it can be argued that during the final weeks of the campaign, journalists should write more fully and more frequently about challengers than we have observed. Some type of "catch-up" coverage, spotlighting challengers, is necessary. This means that reporters must work harder: it is considerably less taxing to unearth the educational backgrounds of two candidates than to sort out their differences on nuclear power plants or agricultural policy, for example.

The burden of responsibility falls on others as well. Our data suggest at least two additional antidotes for the weaknesses we diagnose. First, the process of candidate recruitment must be more fully examined in light of weakened party organizations. Fowler (1979) sees decisions to run for Congress as analogous to participating in a lottery; not unexpectedly, the probability of winning becomes critical in determining the types of candidates who ultimately choose to enter the race. Most congressional districts present bleak electoral possibilities to newcomers, and this must have a significant effect on the types of candidates who can be persuaded to seek congressional office. Popular stereotypes suggest that House candidates tend to two types: politically ambitious attorneys and party dullards. Though stereotypes overstate the case, we must think seriously about the kinds of candidates willing to enter hopeless races against members of Congress.

Second, reporters, particularly those covering close races, should be aware that they may unwittingly fall prey to habits of preferential coverage of incumbents. Exposing differences between candidates can generate conflict in news columns, which may breed readership. Aggressive reporting can be in a newspaper's self-interest, and might, across several elections, stimulate citizen involvement.

This discussion sidesteps the issue of how much competition is essential. Certainly we are not implying that close races should occur in all districts every two years. But the number of sacrificial candidates indicates that there is not "enough" competition. To be sure, impressive victories could be a tribute to current officeholders; but the evidence suggests rather that voters have not been presented with meaningful alternatives.

High and continuous turnover could work against sound government. The House requires experienced members to attend to its business in an efficient and effective manner. But most observers would agree that representatives should be responsive to voters. Perhaps incumbents would continue to be reelected even if the level of visibility among challengers was relatively high. One would be much more sanguine about congressional responsiveness if this were in fact the case.

Wholesale change in the political landscape does not come easily or quickly. We have mentioned overhauls in recruitment incentives and party structure; this report has few suggestions concerning those issues. Newspaper coverage is not the only key to understanding the processes involved in House races; but more self-conscious monitoring of candidates' coverage in news columns might help compensate for the many advantages that accrue to incumbents.

V

Muted Voices on the Editorial Page

ESSAYS AND BIOGRAPHIES concerned with the press depict the editorial page as a stage where high journalistic drama is played. Lords of the media—the McCormicks, Hearsts, Pulitzers—carved their roles in history with election endorsements and controversial positions staunchly asserted. No less the case for famous editors. John Oakes of the *New York Times* believes editorial pages to be "the 'soul' of newspapers, reflections of their inner character and philosophy" (Talese 1969: 97). It is no accident that men and women with strong opinions and egos gravitate to these assignments; clashes and accommodations between editorial writers and powerful publishers make suspenseful reading.

From this literature one might imagine that congressional endorsements in the nation's press ring with vigorous language. Survey and content analysis paint a different and sobering picture of the newspaper's opinion functions.

The Characteristics and Importance of Editorial Endorsements

Our scrutiny begins with the fact that many newspapers do not endorse political candidates. Among major-circulation dailies in our congressional districts, one in ten has a policy against endorsing any candidate, for any office. One in five of the remaining papers planned not to endorse a House contender or had not made a decision by the time we contacted the editor (within two weeks of election day).*

Most of the indecision or reluctance to endorse a candidate is found in incumbent/challenger contests. In these races, papers champion no one's cause in 30 percent of the cases. Where an outright recommendation is made, more than 90 percent support incumbents.

A lack of resolve to editorialize seems puzzling. Where is the lionhearted press, eager to play its role as public watchdog, member of the Fourth Estate? Is it reticence, timidity, lack of news value, or boredom that stays the editorial pen?

Boredom seems unlikely. Refusal to provide editorial support is most common in elections decided by the narrowest margins. Five of 11 papers covering close contests decided not to favor one side, compared with about two in ten of those covering less competitive races. An unflattering interpretation of this finding would question journalistic courage. Perhaps it is embarrassing to be caught supporting the losing side.

Any illusions about literary flourishes in editorials can also be laid to rest. The use of language and argument is more routine than bold.† Indeed, in about one in ten cases, a paper's stand is merely a laundry list of preferred candidates. Congressional contenders are hidden in a typographic thicket among judges, senators, ballot propositions, and the like.‡

Most of the remaining editorials can be lumped into two nearly equal stacks. One type is the short blurb voicing support for an incumbent; the other is an extended argument telling readers about both candidates.

---

*Coombs, in an analysis of Senate and gubernatorial races, found that "a number of newspapers did not endorse any candidate for office; rates of uncommitted stances in contested elections range from 21 percent to 32 percent." He estimates that "14 percent of all papers taking the uncommitted stance do so out of general policy considerations" (MacKuen and Coombs 1981: 186). In a study of nondaily newspapers, Hynds and Martin (1979) found that only 44 percent endorse at the local level.

†Thrift (1977) measures "editorial vigor" by four criteria. An editorial should (1) be about a local topic, (2) use the argumentative form, (3) be controversial, and (4) provide mobilizing information.

‡Where papers print detailed statements of endorsement and follow on the Sunday or Monday before election day with a simple list, we have read the longer pieces for completeness and quality of argument.

The blurb endorsement takes on a numbing familiarity from Seattle to Newark, Charleston to San Diego: "[The incumbent] has compiled a good record in Congress, and [the challenger] offers no effective alternative." Period.

Occasionally, a sliver of detail about the House member will be added, rarely any about the opponent. The incumbent may have "worked hard on urban problems," or "combined practical judgment with progressive inclinations," or "fit well with the rest of the congressional delegation," or "showed signs of having received the message that most citizens want less government adventurism of the kind requiring inflationary federal spending."

Now and then, blurbs describe the unendorsed challenger as a "respectable opponent" or as "failing to mount an aggressive campaign." But this is as far as they venture; challengers are almost never analyzed beyond some statement about the quality of their campaign or about their personal characteristics.

We are not surprised that the blurb endorsement is most common in large metropolitan papers. The spread of population during the past 30 years, from compact cities to suburbs oozing along freeway arteries, has changed the political landscape too. Editorial writers at large papers face many congressional races in their circulation zones; we can sympathize with the urge to save effort by writing conclusions shorn of argument.

But sympathy with the writer's dilemma ought to extend to the plight of eligible voters, who may conclude, from a pattern of blurb editorials across successive congressional elections, that such elections are not particularly important. Voters can be forgiven if they conclude that the election is barely contested, so why should they bother to cast ballots?

Bulletin-like summaries by smaller papers are more difficult to rationalize. They usually take the form of a lazy concession: "We don't especially like the incumbent, but it would be unwise to throw away his/her experience by electing the challenger."

By contrast, many of the lengthy editorials we saw, replete with argument and analysis, are impressive. A metropolitan paper in the West outlines important issues of water and other resource management and keys its endorsements in several races to them. It also covers the various issues at stake and the personal characteristics of the candidates in each of the five races in its circulation zone.

A southern paper recounts a district's political history and contrasts current contenders along liberal-conservative lines. The challenger is liberal; he is also a well-liked writer formerly on the paper. The conservative incumbent gets the nod, however. Though "the district would not be embarrassed by either of these gentlemen," the paper feels "conservative viewpoints are underrepresented in the current Congress." The "interests of better party and ideological balance in the House" win over friendship.

A paper in the industrial Midwest writes a lukewarm and detailed column on the incumbent. His voting record "shows sensitivity" to district needs; his attendance record, "while worse than most, is not terrible"; his services to constituents are "outstanding." Examples are offered to show that the member "talks out of both sides of his mouth," practicing the politics of hypocrisy. "We don't disagree with very many of his votes," the paper concedes, "but we don't think he's ever going to win an award for political candor or political courage." The challenger, despite an energetic and articulate campaign, fails to reap support, because "his philosophy is out of tune with the majority of district voters." He is "not merely a conservative, but a shallow ideologue of the right wing."

A newspaper in upstate New York allots 22 inches and a photograph to the "bright, articulate, and hard-working" incumbent. Ideology and issues distinguish the two candidates. The editorial refers to the government's job-training program, defense expenditures, nuclear power, government spending and tax cuts, the effect of the Kemp-Roth bill on inflation, the responsibilities of governing in a pluralistic democracy, the quality of constituent services and the congressional staff supplying them, Delaware River legislation, airline service to the region, benefits to laid-off industrial workers, the Turkish arms embargo, the Equal Rights Amendment, and the chairing of significant committees. Readers may be dazed trying to keep all these elements sorted into a coherent argument. But there is no questioning the newspaper's attentiveness to congressional politics, its weighing of local concerns along with general political ideology, or its thoughtfulness in comparing the contenders.

A final type of editorial expression deserves comment. We call it support-without-endorsement. It can be found in almost one in every six papers we surveyed. The editorial writer raises an issue—electrical power generation, fiscal restraint, inflation. Sometimes a bill pending in Congress or a recent government report provides the peg. The incumbent's stand on the issue is mentioned, but the column ends without expressing its support for the candidate's reelection. The challenger's name never appears. These pieces are printed on the editorial page; the paper links its judgment and prestige with the incumbent's record, but does not explicitly urge voters to cast their ballot for that candidate. The reader is left to infer that a vote for change would damage the district's interests.

Editorials emerge from this analysis as less vibrant, less muscular statements of purpose than might be imagined from the literature on journalism's giants. But if the product is disappointing, it is nonetheless crafted with high expectations about its importance and influence. We asked political reporters and editorial-page editors a series of questions about what effects they thought an editorial endorsement by their paper might have in a House district race.

Most (90 percent) are convinced endorsements sway independent voters toward the paper's candidate; a large majority (70 to 80 percent) believe that editorials can stir enthusiasm among party members, mobilize volunteers, and pick up votes from the opposite party. Fewer than half (about 40 percent) feel that the columns encourage greater public interest in elections by stimulating turnout.*

Our journalists' trust in the potency of editorial support in

---

*Similarly, most weekly and other nondaily newspaper editors "believe their editorials do exert an influence on their readers. As might be expected, most perceive their greatest influence to be at the local level" (Hynds & Martin 1979: 322).

House races is sustained by research carried out in other electoral spheres. Robinson (1974), after a painstaking analysis of national survey data, concluded that in presidential races, endorsements account for an average 3 percent shift in party-line support. Coombs (MacKuen & Coombs 1981) suggests that a newspaper's support of gubernatorial or senatorial candidates can influence as many as 20 percent of the voters to defect from their party.*

A paradox appears to be operating here. Journalists, by and large, think editorials influence the political process. But newspapers are often timid about venturing into hotly contested races, and the endorsements they do make often lack assertiveness, argumentative quality, or literary style. These journalists seem to back away from a strong, overt exercise of their influence.

The Endorsement Process

To examine how newspaper organizations come to their conclusions about endorsement, we asked editors about their decision-making process.

The steps by which endorsement decisions are reached have rarely been studied, and only in connection with dramatic campaigns (e.g., Swanberg 1961; Halberstam 1979). The intricate play of opinions, information exchange, and influence within newspapers is difficult to unravel from the outside. Contacts between a district's political activists and the press extend across months and years. One-shot interviews with editors can hardly hope to cast more than an unrefined light on the endorsement process.

The broad outlines of this sequence of events can be given shape, however. Editors answered a series of questions about preparatory work (such as interviewing candidates), about individuals who had "contributed ideas before the decision was reached," and about staff members who had "the most influence" in making the final candidate choice.

---

*Others have found that editorials make a substantial difference in election contests for President (Erikson 1976), state representative (Mason 1973), mayor (McClenghan 1973), and county district attorney (Scarrow & Borman 1979).

Decision-making processes differ across newspapers in important ways. The question concerning "the most influential person" provides a revealing glimpse into the politics of editorializing. We recorded job titles of the key actor in each organization, permitting us to sort newspapers into four categories:

1. Papers where the key actor was a *news executive*—an editor, managing editor, political editor, or the like.

2. Papers where the key actor was a *business executive*—a publisher, owner, general manager.

3. Papers where the key actor was a *group*; sometimes this was formalized as an "editorial board," and elsewhere editors referred to "collective decisions" or "consensus."

4. Papers where the key actor was the *editorial-page editor* or an *editorial writer*.

The 42 papers we surveyed divide across endorsement styles as follows:

News executive	38%
Business executive	26
Group	24
Editorial-page editor/staff	12

One could argue in behalf of any of these endorsement styles. Those who want to protect the editorial side against encroachments from the business side will like organizations where a news executive takes the reins. That person, higher in the bureaucracy than the editorial-page editor, can more effectively battle with the business side. People who subscribe to hierarchical management will prefer the decision making to be done by business executives, who are closest to the top of the organization and are responsible for the paper's public image in the community. Fans of participatory management will like group decisions, especially editorial boards combining representatives from several of the paper's departments. And finally, those fond of departmental autonomy within bureaucracies will favor decision making by the editorial-page editor or staff.

The effort or seriousness a newspaper shows in reaching its decision is reflected in the kind of information it gathers beforehand. We lack an absolute standard to sift good decisions from poor ones; but we can distinguish between purposeful and casual decision-making processes. Interviewing the candidates is the most obvious place to start. Seven of ten editors said "the paper had talked with the incumbent," and eight of ten reported some "time with the challenger."

Editors also recounted other discussions—with campaign managers and aides, party leaders, government officials, or groups supporting candidates. About one in three papers relied on additional sources like these before making an endorsement. This figure undoubtedly overlooks the many occasions when information seeps gratuitously into the decision-making process—from casual encounters between journalists or business management and sources.

A rough measure of pre-endorsement effort combines contact with candidates and other sources into a single index. A newspaper earns the highest score by interviewing both contenders and one other person.

Table 7 shows the average amount of effort at papers by endorsement style. The greatest work transpires where endorsements are governed by business executives and editorial-page staff. Places where decisions are made by groups score lowest on the pre-decision search for information that could lend rationality and coherence to editorial stands.

These findings will not comfort journalists who believe in a church/state-like separation between editorial and business functions. But the results make sense in terms of organizational theory (Katz & Kahn 1966): care is invested in decisions where top management participates. A high score was also registered by the small number of papers where editorial-page editors make the endorsement decisions. Perhaps the undivided attention these journalists can devote to articulating the newspaper's positions explains their superior showing.

None of these results speaks to the political "wisdom" expressed in endorsements or to their literary merits. Well-researched endorsements can be foolish or written in unappealing style. But it is difficult to imagine snap decisions being wise or insightful. In this primitive sense, hard work—

TABLE 7

Pre-Decision Effort at 42 Newspapers, by Endorsement Style

Endorsement style	Average activity score (1–4)
News executive	1.7
Business executive	2.3
Group	1.4
Editorial-page editor/staff	2.4

NOTE: Newspapers receive credit for each of the electoral participants interviewed. 1 = no pre-endorsement effort; 2 = interview with one person (candidate, campaign aide, government official, member of endorsing group); 3 = interview with two people; 4 = interview with both candidates and one other person.

that is, pre-decision interviewing—may be credited as an index of organizational quality.

Our description of the cast on stage during endorsement decision making would not be complete without mentioning a journalistic actor hidden in the wings. Our interviews with editors included questions about the role of supporting players. Many on the editorial-page staff, in the business office, or among news executives were mentioned as contributors to the paper's final decision. But one figure was conspicuously missing: the reporter who covers the House races; the person in the front-row seats is rarely consulted. After probing up to five times, we extracted 124 descriptions of staff members who "contributed ideas before endorsements were made": only 11 of these were reporters.* This strange neglect of an organizational resource adds to an already mixed picture of decision making.†

We cannot say why reporters are so invisible. Perhaps the remoteness of editorial department offices, separated from

*Reporters are just as invisible in open races, where candidates are least known and where daily intelligence from the campaign trail might be most helpful.

†In a survey of editorial-page editors, Hynds and Martin (1977) found that many (77 percent) editors cite reporters who covered the topic of the editorials as an information source, though not necessarily a participant in the endorsement process.

newsrooms at so many papers, is one explanation. Another, even more charitable explanation, goes like this: editorial-page editors fear that asking newspeople about a campaign would put the reporters' standards of objectivity in jeopardy, drawing them into a compromising relationship with the paper's opinion function. That is possible in individual cases. But the general pattern of the relationship between editorials and news suggests otherwise. The internal use of a reporter's information for reaching an endorsement decision hardly seems as potentially embarrassing as a demonstrably imbalanced journalistic effort (see below).

What, finally, can be said about the opinion function of newspapers? We have already established that many papers abstain from making endorsements in House races, and that where endorsements are made, almost all support incumbents. Furthermore, with some exceptions, editorials lack intellectual substance; they offer thin argumentative gruel. Now we can add that in six of ten papers the style of reaching endorsement decisions entails a minimum of work. And at almost no paper does the editorial-page editor claim to have consulted reporters, who follow candidates during their vote-seeking gyrations. It is hard to reconcile this casualness in performance with the widespread belief in the journalistic community that endorsements make a difference in the political process.

Editorial Stand and News Play

Among the many popular impressions about the press, perhaps the most damning is the ancient chestnut that editorial and news functions are intermingled. In political races the suspicious, cynical, or perhaps just observant citizen is often led to charge that newspapers tailor their news coverage to suit their endorsement preferences. Thundering denials are heard from the journalistic community (Sanoff 1975).

These quarrels usually lack a reasonable definition of bias; models of "fair" news treatment are hard to construct. When one candidate receives more attention than another, the cause might be found in more energetic campaigning rather than journalistic manipulation. Vigorous and adept campaigners may be more astute politically, more newsworthy, and more likely to win a deserved endorsement.

The concept of bias implies an ideological compatibility between officeseeker and media management. We suspect this pales in comparison to the advantages of incumbency that our study has already illuminated. We favor less presumptive language for examining the relationships between editorial stand and news play—let us say the potential for "concurrence" between a newspaper's two voices.

Settling questions in the popular mind is not our only reason for looking at the possible links between endorsements and news play. Earlier we cited some of the evidence turned up by other researchers looking into the impact of editorial stand on voters' candidate choices. That evidence seems to sustain the view of journalists that endorsements make a difference. But the research results are open to another explanation: what if endorsement is strongly related to imbalanced news coverage? If so, might not the treatment accorded candidates in heavily read news pages account for the bulk of the influence imputed to the press?

In studying editorial and news "concurrence" in House elections we are hindered by the fact that few papers endorsed challengers; we are forced to compare papers that take no stand against those that endorse incumbents. And it is helpful to look separately at tight races and the less competitive ones. The closest contests represent our best crucible for testing imbalanced coverage; candidates are most equally matched in resources, and most likely to merit equal news attention, regardless of who the paper's favorite is.

Table 8 tells the story. It shows the median number of additional paragraphs written about incumbents compared with challengers. A dramatic pattern emerges in tight races. Incumbents were accorded advantages in news play generally, but especially where they also won the paper's endorsement. In those cases the typical incumbent got 32 more paragraph mentions than the challenger.

In other, less competitive races newspapers endorsing in-

TABLE 8

Median Incumbent Advantage in News Copy, by Competitiveness of Race and Newspaper's Endorsement Stand

Type of race	Incumbent advantage in news copy	No. of papers
Tight races[a]		
No endorsement[b]	15	5
Endorse incumbent	32	6
Other races		
No endorsement[b]	2	8
Endorse incumbent	16	34

NOTE: The advantage figures were calculated by subtracting the number of paragraphs about challengers from the number of paragraphs about incumbents.

[a]Elections having outcomes in the 42–58 percent range.

[b]Papers not making House endorsements, but having no policy against candidate endorsements.

cumbents gave their choice about 16 more paragraphs than they gave the challengers. Where no endorsement was extended, coverage was nearly equal.

One lesson is clear. Where the competition for office is most intense, news attention and editorial-page support are tied firmly together. Without deeper probing, we cannot say that our results point to some collusion by newspapers to protect the political careers of those they favor. But regardless of the causes, press performance undoubtedly dampens any hopes for a certain amount of electoral turnover. Journalistic barriers against political change are set on the high side indeed.

Our findings serve as a warning about the conclusions that have been drawn from studies of the effects of editorial endorsements. At least at the House level, imbalanced news coverage seems a more plausible influence on the voter. As we have seen, many of the endorsements are thin and poorly crafted statements. Paragraphs of news coverage about the incumbent appear where readers seek other news and entertainment, are spread across many days during the campaign, and carry the mantle of objective reporting.

Discussion

We touch on three themes that recur in discussions of the editorial impact of newspapers (Shaw 1977). Most importantly, we can confirm a relationship between endorsement and news play. The winning of editorial-page support may or may not sway voters; its correlation with preferential news reporting, however, cannot be denied.

The bulk of editorials make dull reading indeed. If opinion pages once resounded with fact and flourish, they seldom do so now.

Partisanship in editorializing takes on a slightly different meaning and significance; incumbency in itself appears to be more important than party affiliation, at least in congressional elections.

We cannot measure whether endorsements swing any weight among voters in congressional races, especially as compared with more prominent races, until there is a larger pool of challenger endorsements to study. That day seems far off. In the meantime, we need to look at the importance of endorsements from another angle: how does this expression of elite approval aid fund raising, grease access to reporters' notebooks, and give credibility to a campaign?

The Voters' Understanding
of Candidates

THUS FAR we have appraised press performance in House races from the journalistic side. In this chapter we examine what the newspaper-reading public knows about congressional candidates. More specifically, we compare the respective roles of press coverage and partisan campaigning in shaping voters' images of candidates.

It is not easy to arrive at an appropriate criterion for comparing the effects of journalism and paid persuasion. Ideally, the one seeks to stimulate reflection based on facts, and the other to mobilize quick and unswerving support.

Public understanding is an appealing standard by which to gauge campaign impact. Democratic electoral processes assume a reasoning citizenry—people who make political choices on the basis of known features of the alternatives (Clarke & Fredin 1978). It is the assignment of the journalist, among other duties, to inform. Increasingly, this teaching process takes place amid the blare of partisan appeals that use technologically and psychologically sophisticated strategies.

Recent developments in psychology point to an efficient, theoretically sound way to elicit what people know about candidates (Zajonc 1980). People's feelings about things—candidates, products, and acquaintances—may be independent from the "facts" that are thought to be known about them. Feelings may be acquired before other types of information and may be used to categorize information. This is especially likely in the case of political figures who are distant from the daily concerns of most people.*

It makes sense to retrieve what the public knows by asking people what they like and dislike about candidates. Open or free-response questions invite eligible voters to offer the most salient characteristics that they think of in connection with a given candidate. This information-storage system anchored to feelings about the candidate squares well with the voters' task at the polls, where they render a single and unchangeable choice. Some of the things people "know" about candidates may not survive the test of independent validation. But how they feel about candidates, their likes and dislikes, surely enter into their final choice.

Fortunately, a probability sample of the electorate in each of our congressional districts is available from the National Election Study (ICPSR 1979). Interviewers contacted registered voters immediately after the election; questions covered media-use patterns, candidate choices, and a broad range of political topics.†

Our analysis of that survey reveals three features of press performance relating to the subject we are most interested in: the competition for congressional office. Two of our findings encourage one's faith in newspapers as a significant American institution:

1. News coverage of candidates affects public awareness about them even when the level of campaign spending is held constant.

---

*As Zajonc states, "Decisions about affect require least information and they are often based on a different decision scheme than either recognition or feature identification. Each of the three, affect, recognition, and feature identification, is a form of categorization. Affective reactions of the type considered here are for the most part unidimensional and sometimes just binary: safe-dangerous, good-bad, or nice-nasty. Such binary decisions can under some circumstances be made quite reliably, even in the absence of reliable bases" (p. 171). This conception of perception dovetails nicely with findings about the relatively low level of public attentiveness to congressional campaigns.

†The NES data were released by the Inter-university Consortium for Political and Social Research, which is not responsible for any interpretations that appear here.

2. Press performance is especially critical in tight races, where incumbents face strong, well-financed challengers.

Beyond these findings, however, stands an ominous one:

3. In open races, where the prospects seem brightest for competition, the press virtually ignores candidates. These contenders' ability to capture public attention depends on how much they can raise and spend for their messages.

Methods

The previous chapters have been based on interviews at newspapers with the largest daily circulation in their districts. Now our interest shifts to the connection between press performance and public information. To gather voter-linked data, we identified the newspaper with the largest daily penetration reaching the Primary Sampling Unit (PSU) where the NES interviews were conducted.* Sometimes both district and PSU criteria were met by the same paper, and sometimes they were not.

Results in this chapter are based on data from 82 newspapers, 71 incumbent/challenger races, and 11 open races. This analysis examines news articles ($N = 653$), and includes each of the 4,071 paragraphs where the candidate's name or reference appeared.

Voters' Likes and Dislikes

Interviews uncovered candidate information in a direct manner. People were asked whether there was anything they liked or disliked about each contender and if so, what it was. All pieces of information were coded into an elaborate set of content categories.

---

*Survey staff obtained an average of 25 personal interviews in each congressional district. Ideally, household sampling would have distributed voter interviews throughout the entire district; this could not be done because of financial limitations. When the congressional district was part of a major city, its sample of eight to ten interview clusters was distributed across the district. But with lower population density, the sample was confined to a part of the district's geographic area, which was randomly drawn; this was the Primary Sampling Unit. Selected households were spread within the PSU according to probability sampling procedures—with the understanding that such selection could never mirror the heterogeneity of the district or serve as a basis for precise district estimates.

Few voters spontaneously offer features of a purely political nature. Officeseekers are thought to be good or bad, decisive or weak, honest or dishonest, hard-working or lazy, likable or disagreeable. This coincides with Zajonc's ordering of affect before cognition. But though respondents rarely start with the candidate's stand on issues, ideology, or group ties, we unearth abundant evidence about these political features when our inquiry scratches more deeply. We will return to this point shortly.

Not surprisingly, earlier research on voters' perceptions of candidates has been rooted in presidential politics (Kinder 1976, 1978; Fiske & Kinder 1979; Kinder et al. 1979). National campaigns whip up the attention of large numbers of citizens who are marginally informed about the candidates. The role of party identification—in forming candidate images as well as preferences—has been celebrated across decades of surveys.

If we pursue this party-based mode of analysis at the House level, familiar evidence about the structure of candidate images emerges.* How much one likes the Democrat correlates negatively with favorable views about the Republican. Candidate dislikes, on the contrary, correlate positively; when people criticize, they tend to find ill in both officeseekers.

But Congress differs from the presidential stage in many ways; most importantly for us, party identification recedes in favor of incumbency as the most important ingredient in the voter's choice. Implications for press performance can best be traced by noting differences in the voters' images of officeholders and their challengers.

A first glance at these images discloses striking differences in the public's awareness. Incumbents not only are well known, but are much better liked than their challengers. Among 988 newspaper readers, 54 percent have a positive bit of information about the sitting members of the House, compared with just 10 percent for their opponents. This imbalance is not re-

*The following inquiry is confined to eligible voters who read daily newspapers. This provides a view of political beliefs among more attentive citizens.

flected in dislikes. Challengers and incumbents alike draw the same proportion of critical mentions—16 percent.*

Stokes and Miller, in their classic analysis of midterm congressional elections (1966), concluded that "recognition carries a positive valence; to be perceived at all is to be perceived favorably" (p. 205). Evidence from our analysis of the 1978 NES data departs from this view in the case of challengers. This contrast acquires special significance for press behavior when we look into the links between candidate images and voter support.

For incumbents, experienced actors on the electoral stage, the public's likes and dislikes correlate with the voting outcome in the customary way. The more favorable the impression, the more ballot support (Tau = .32); the more negative the impression, the less the support (Tau = −.41).

Challengers are a different breed, however. They are living evidence of the aptness of the slogan attributed to publicity-starved celebrities: "I don't care what you write about me, as long as you spell my name right." People who have positive things to say about challengers are more likely to vote for them (Tau = .38); but so are people with critical or unfavorable impressions (Tau = .41).

The trench from which challengers must wage their electoral warfare takes on clearer dimensions from these results. They are relatively unknown, of course. What the public knows is more likely to be negative than positive. This may result, partly, from quick judgments made on the basis of the incumbents' greater news play and greater budgets for partisan messages.

The canny challenger begs for press attention of any kind. "Cover the candidates' joint appearance before the League of Women Voters" ("Even if I come across as less assured or knowledgeable," the challenger might reason, "I'll become better known and more electable"). "Interview me as well as the incumbent before deciding once again to endorse him or

---

*In one respect, candidates in open races occupy a midground between challengers and incumbents: 30 percent in the NES survey found something to like about the candidates, and 17 percent something to dislike. Perhaps there is a bedrock of about one in six eligible voters following the news who finds something unappealing about any officeseeker.

her" ("Though you may not like my political style or positions, sentences about me may wander onto your editorial page"). "Assign a reporter to cover me for a day on the campaign trail" ("Even chilly receptions at plant gates can translate into attention—possibly into sympathetic copy").

There are limits to the value of negative publicity for challengers; beyond some point, dislikes breed rejection, as the data for the incumbents show. In fact, the challengers' most obvious strategy, beyond attempting to boost their name recognition, is to capitalize on the tendency of voters to translate their dislikes about an incumbent into a No vote at the polls: find a vulnerable spot in the House member's image, publicize it, and hope it catches fire with voters.

The implications for press treatment of challengers are clear; at the bare threshold of public awareness where most lie, candidacies ignored by newspapers are doomed. With coverage, the public can at least see and consider challengers. Of course, this visibility might reveal inadequacies as well as merits. And though few candidates may actually unseat members of the House, this visibility would probably bring them more votes and increase electoral competition.

We now turn to a question raised earlier, and shelved. Does the public link issue stands with House elections? When casting their ballots, do citizens consider taxes, employment, defense, social welfare, education, transportation, environmental protection, or any other concerns that divide and unite voting blocs?

At first blush, the answer would seem to be no. Free responses about candidates' likes and dislikes fail to show much policy or programmatic content. But after all, the National Election Study asked how contenders were viewed as persons; we should not be startled to find newspaper readers answering in kind.

When the interviewers pressed on, asking about "issues important in the House district campaign," people came up with a raft of important problems facing the country. The list resembled any roster of ailments in the body politic, and in 1978 was dominated by economic concerns—taxes, employment, inflation, and the like. Social welfare issues also appeared. And almost one in ten newspaper readers cites the quality of leadership in government, the credibility of public agencies, or other facets of the functioning of the political system. Only a handful of eligible voters failed to name an issue associated with the House election.

To be sure, the depth of the voters' concern is open to question. Perhaps the interview simply unearths a standard agenda of current affairs, to which Presidents, Popes, and members of the House are expected to respond. Yet we are led to infer otherwise. There are signs that the public does take a considerable interest in Congress's handling of policy and programs.

Some past research encourages this unconventional view. Wright, for example, noted in his study of the policy positions of candidates (1978: 456):

Contrary to much of the literature, the voters behave as though they are attentive to candidates; the stands candidates take on issues have been shown to affect the manner in which voters make electoral decisions. Relative proximity and issue distances between candidates are found to have clear effects on party defections, the impact of incumbency, and the influence of voter issue preferences on voting in House elections. . . . Even if the majority of the electorate is largely oblivious to candidates and their policy actions, we do not need to conclude that issues are unimportant in House elections. As long as issue-oriented voters are reasonably dispersed throughout the electorate and they influence a significant portion of votes of other less concerned voters, House elections can be effective, even if somewhat loose, means of popular control over representatives and public policy.

Songer (1981) agrees. Between one-third and one-half of the voters in the two Oklahoma districts he studied could correctly identify their representative's roll-call vote, depending on the issue. (These figures were corrected for respondents' guessing.) Under the circumstances, he concluded that it would be rash for House members to cast a vote in the belief that their stand does not matter to the electorate. One could infer with equal confidence that the press's coverage of issues is valued information among the involved citizens who cast ballots in congressional races.

The NES data can be used to extend this point. When respondents named an issue, they were asked whether they tended to prefer one of the candidates because of it. Voters' use of issues in making their candidate choice correlates strongly (Tau = .47) with their knowledge of other characteristics of the candidate. People who were well informed (i.e., those who offered several likes and dislikes) about the contenders said they relied on issues to make up their minds.

We add an important detail. A respondent's conscious use of issues in making a candidate choice is also linked to his or her use of the press or other media to follow the campaign. From this and the previous finding we draw a novel, if humble, conclusion: one can underestimate the degree of concern about the issues among attentive citizens in House elections. Public policy—and its coverage in the press—may matter after all.*

We agree with others who argue that the personal characteristics of public officials can affect how they vote on policy; there is no denying that these qualities have journalistic and political merit. But where newspaper readers can find little policy-oriented information about their favorite or the opposition, they are left to make circumstantial estimates about what will happen to taxes, defense, the environment, and other matters, depending on whether the incumbent is returned or unseated. The journalistic craft, in our opinion, can rise to greater substantive heights. We find a solid base of empirical evidence suggesting that it needs to.

We can now see that the public images of candidates represent a more complex standard of judging media effects than might be thought. Much of what people know lies deeper than the blunt pick and shovel of open-end questions and of survey analysis confined to descriptive percentages.

Journalistic Effort, News Play, Money, and Voters' Understanding

By now it is clear that we favor the airing of public issues. But in probing the impact of the press and campaigning on

---

*See Chapter Three, where we document that many issues vanish between campaigns as candidates wage them and campaigns as they are portrayed by the media.

voters' understanding, we retreat to a less prejudiced standard. It is based on the first things respondents say when asked what they like or dislike about contenders.*

Figure 4d conveys this level of voter understanding for incumbents (I), challengers (C), and candidates in an open contest (O). The figure also shows how vigorously reporters pursued each type of candidate (4a); how many news mentions each received (4b); and how much money each spent in the primary and general election (4c).

Challengers, as we have already seen, are comparatively invisible (4d). One quick but unwise interpretation: challengers have made less of a dent in the electorate's mind because they are new to the public scene. A glance at the median information score for open candidates casts doubt on the "new faces" explanation. Most of these contenders are babes on the congressional stage too, but they have managed to make themselves known. We will shortly see how they accomplished this feat, and how small a role professional journalism played in the process.

We turn to two major forces that can influence public understanding: news and advertising.† In Figure 4a we see that reporters exert about equal energy traipsing after incumbents and challengers—talking to the candidates, phoning their managers, digging in the library or newspaper morgue, and the rest. But this equality of effort does not translate into an equality of news coverage as shown in 4b. Incumbents get greater coverage, receiving 25 paragraphs against the challengers' 16.

---

*We simply summed the number of discretely coded likes and dislikes that each eligible voter (also newspaper reader) associated with each of the candidates in his or her district.

†It is important to keep in mind that news paragraphs and total campaign expenditures are not comparable measures. Regardless of the types of articles written, news paragraph is a fairly standard measure across all districts. But the total of campaign expenditures does not have this appealing simplicity. There is no fixed equation between dollars spent and media purchases. Other analyses (e.g., Goldenberg & Traugott 1979) find that media outlays account for approximately 40 percent of the typical congressional candidate's budget. We proceed by assuming that advertising represents a constant proportion of total budget. A larger coffer provides an opportunity for more media buys and also for hiring staff who are adroit at handling media decisions.

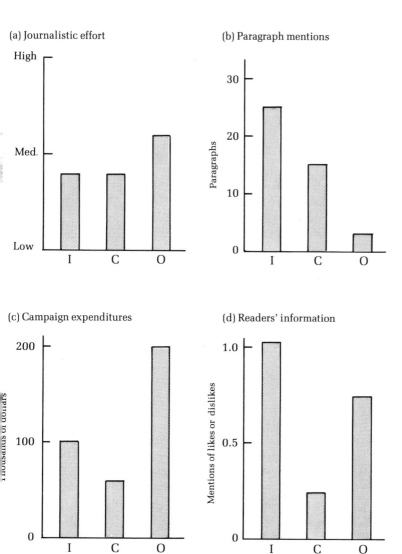

(a) Journalistic effort

High

Med.

Low

  I   C   O

(b) Paragraph mentions

Paragraphs

30

20

10

0

  I   C   O

(c) Campaign expenditures

Thousands of dollars

200

100

0

  I   C   O

(d) Readers' information

Mentions of likes or dislikes

1.0

0.5

0

  I   C   O

Fig. 4. Median level of journalistic effort, number of paragraph mentions, amount of campaign spending, and level of readers' information in 71 incumbent/challenger races and 11 open races. I is incumbent, C is challenger, and O is candidate in an open race.

Incumbents also outspend challengers by a significant margin, as Figure 4c makes clear. And their money does double duty for them: it fuels their campaigns and it brings advantages in news value. The difference in the number of paragraphs for each incumbent/challenger contest correlates strongly with the amount of the incumbent's expenditures; the more a member spends, the wider the gap that he or she enjoys over the challenger in news play. In contrast, spending by the challenger does not correlate with equality in press attention; successful fund raising by the newcomer does not help close the gap.

Open races present an even more obvious test of political competition. Two candidates, usually unmatched against each other in previous races, vie for public attention on a relatively equal footing; the outcomes of these contests are generally closer than those involving incumbents. The press should be drawn to matches with fresh contenders, lavish spending, and less predictable outcomes.

The data tell a different story. Reporters work harder to cover open candidates than they do in covering incumbents and challengers. But this produces a disappointingly thin file of published stories. Open races are almost invisible in public print. An unmistakable political story fails to command newshole.

But if editors and publishers are indifferent, newspaper readers are very much alive to open campaigns. The median information score for the 22 open candidacies is three times greater than the score for challengers. How can we account for this public awareness? Easily—by noting the campaign dollars spent promoting the interests of open candidates.

As Figure 4c makes clear, these candidates spent twice as much money as the 71 incumbents and four times as much as the 71 challengers. These data offer presumptive evidence that paid advertising reaps dividends.

We test this presumption directly. The 22 open candidacies can be arrayed by size of budget and level of public information. The relationship is steep and linear, with only four deviant cases. In two districts—one in Texas, the other in California—competitors on both sides spent huge amounts of money and gained little public awareness for their efforts. Aside from this quartet, there is little room for any factor except campaign budgets to explain the public's level of information.* If journalism were boosting the public's understanding, we would find campaigns spending small sums but attaining high levels of information. There are no cases of this kind in our 1978 sample.†

So journalism loses again. The stage was set for political change; an incumbent had died, resigned, been driven from office in the primary, or sought other office. New faces were at hand, stimulating reporting activity. But what came of this effort? Almost nothing in the way of published news columns. The 22 candidacies produced a total of 30 news stories between late September and Election Day.

Meanwhile, PACs and other interested parties were pumping money into the districts, with great effect; public attention was won. Candidate preferences were formed without the aid of independent and dispassionate press reports.

In each of the 11 races an incumbent was born. The next time out, he or she can count on being sustained by all the journalistic perquisites we have already documented. In the next election a challenger trying to unseat the one-term officeholder can expect to suffer the same press treatment, invisibility in the news pages and no endorsement on the editorial page. Political competition will suffer another in a repeated series of journalistic blows.

Journalism Versus Money

Well before the campaign starts, voters have accumulated information about incumbents. Hence, it comes as no surprise that relationships between information and two predic-

---

*The correlation between money and public information is .84 without the four deviant candidates. When we include them, the correlation drops to .54.

†We examined the open races on a number of standard criteria. Districts span the country geographically and include newspapers with daily circulations ranging from 6,000 to 555,000. There is no reason to suspect that our results are a fluke arising from special features of these races in 1978.

tors—amount of news reporting this season and size of campaign war chest—are low. Journalistic and monetary output add only marginally to what the public already knows from the representative's years of service.

The voters' information about challengers never catches up to that about incumbents. But the levels of public awareness are quite tightly linked to the amount of press coverage and of campaign dollars invested. How else, except through news reporting and advertising, could citizens learn about challengers, most of whom were visible for the first time in late 1978?

To sharpen this analysis of how news and advertising affect public knowledge, we ask two further questions. The first refinement compares the informing power of news columns with the blast of campaign advertising: does journalistic output explain any part of what the public knows when competing against the wealth of campaign spending? The second refinement is to ask this question separately for tight elections and for shoo-in victories.* Like the open races, close contests stand apart as an opportunity for political change. Participants often anticipate a narrow outcome, leading to greater effort in campaign tactics and in news coverage.

The statistical technique of multiple regression is our tool for this analysis. In trying to understand how much voters know about the candidate, we compared the effect of name mentions in the news to campaign dollars.

The outcome justifies our fascination with press performance. Even in the face of campaign spending, press attention is strongly related to the public's understanding about both incumbents and challengers in tight races, and about challengers in lopsided contests. For the statistically minded, partial beta weights between press coverage and public information are .32 for incumbents and .33 for challengers in tight races, and .36 for challengers who eventually lost by wide margins (all significant). Not surprisingly, neither press cov-

---

*For this analysis, the 71 incumbent/challenger races are divided into tight and lopsided elections at the median. The losers in tight elections drew at least 33 percent.

erage nor the amount of campaign dollars spent predicts how much eligible voters know about incumbents who trounced their opposition.*

There is an additional point to be made about this power of the press. It is found in widely differing journalistic settings. News coverage made a difference in cases where incumbents faced stiff opposition and attracted 39 mentions; where challengers made a strong bid and were mentioned 27 times; and where challengers fell far short of victory and received only 4 mentions. In each of these cases, the partial correlation between news attention and public information is strong, holding campaign dollars constant.†

Campaign expenditures are not without influence. We have already noted their strong correlation with what voters know about candidates in open races. The partial beta for challengers in tight races (controlling for press coverage) is also significant (.48). Campaign money does not correlate with voters' information in any of the other types of candidacies.

Discussion

Public awareness is a product of many communication systems. Media reports intersect with partisan campaigning; both stimulate discussions within families and across backyard fences. Voters' contact with the campaigns on one day provokes further information seeking and media use later. In this chapter, we have focused on two major sources of influence: newspapers and campaign advertising.

On the one hand, we are cheered by results that highlight journalism's power in contributing to the public's understanding of candidates. Yet our findings also paint a side of

---

*Our measure of voters' information about candidates goes well beyond name familiarity. Using that more primitive level of knowledge, Jacobson (1981a) finds weak effects for press coverage, compared with campaign spending. Our results restore confidence in journalistic impact.

†Objections can be raised to our use of multiple regression; the number of candidacies is low, and variables are not distributed ideally for applying this powerful technique. In our defense, there is no more attractive means for trying to distinguish journalistic from advertising effectiveness. We recognize that it is impossible to untangle the indirect effects of campaign coffers, purchasing talented press aides who maneuver a candidacy so as to attract attention in the news.

journalism that cramps political competition. Challengers' access to voters rests on a press coverage that they rarely attract. The avoidance of news about open races by many newspapers forces those candidates to rely on the lubricating flow of campaign dollars, many awarded by PACs and other interest groups.

Why do papers act in these ways? It seems that journalism shrinks from uncertain outcomes in the political realm as though two rules were being followed: (1) when the outcome is in doubt, support the traditional winner; (2) when the electoral prize will be won by a newcomer in an open race, stay away from the contest—do not risk identifying with a loser. These rules stand as a dark translation of our findings. Safety and timidity are their unifying themes.

The damaging consequences from this kind of press performance can easily be identified. Reluctance to report on candidates hampers the most involved voters in their efforts to distinguish between contenders. Challengers are hindered more than incumbents, and competitors in close elections are especially hurt. The public's education about candidates in open races rests to an extraordinary degree on campaign dollars, leaving little room for influence by the press. The vitality of electoral processes suffers.

Why have newspapers fallen into these habits? How can journalism recover from these practices and exert a more constructive influence on political life? Chapter Seven relates some ideas we have gleaned from newspeople, from candidates, and from political operatives who believe in a vibrant and democratic political system.

New Leads to Political Reporting

THUS FAR we have recounted the actors in electoral journalism and the setting in which it is played. In previous chapters we examined reporters' newsgathering techniques, the selective, judgmental filters through which news events are processed, the unbalanced coverage afforded incumbents in both news and editorial columns, and the effects of newspaper practices on the public's understanding of contenders. Throughout, we have insisted that journalistic behavior be viewed against a larger and changing political landscape. The most prominent features include swelling expenditures, intervention by PACs, and redefined parties with diminished influence.

We want to conclude our study on a constructive note, rather than on a finger-wagging one. Our results paint a grim, even alarming picture of press performance. After the surveys and content analysis were completed, we shared our findings with journalists and political operatives, hereafter called discussants, inviting three contributions:

1. *Do our findings and interpretations seem accountable? Have we mapped terrain between politics and journalism that is utterly unfamiliar or fanciful?*

2. *How do you explain what we have found?*

3. *Have you any recommendations for how media and campaigners can undertake their tasks, improving the qual-*

*ity of political information and encouraging greater compe-
tition for the House?*

Editors, reporters, campaign aides, candidates, and accomplished political observers enthusiastically joined our circle,
convened without the benefit of scientific sampling. Some
findings startled them; others seemed routine. All the results
described a believable if depressing reality. Conversations
across many hours of meetings yielded a rich harvest of suggestions, growing out of our discussants' experiences in the
political process.

We presented that reality in two forms. One was in abstract
terms, drawing on our survey evidence that generalizes to
newspapers and districts nationwide. Though this representative picture has clear advantages for gauging press practices, it lacks the vividness of personal encounters. This second dimension to our results came from studying three
political reporters in depth. Discussants found our case studies a helpful way to capture essentials from surveys and content analysis. We introduce readers to our examples to make
the same point: real people and their reporting behavior
cluster around the averages, the percentages, and the correlations that often seem to spread the distance between research
and reality.*

Three Political Reporters

Tom reports for a 127,000 circulation daily, in a city insulated from competition by any other daily newspaper. We
pick up his story one morning two weeks before the election.

Tom fidgets at his desk, shuffling notes haphazardly. Other
reporters at the *Times* do not notice; they are glued to their
own desks, working on their assignments under deadline
pressure, or flipping through newspapers between sips of
coffee. It is 8:10; Tom needs to write at least six inches of
campaign copy within the hour.

He has been calling around—last night and this morning
—to flesh out a press release issued by the representative of

*The names of reporters and newspapers have been changed to preserve
anonymity.

the Second District, proclaiming his support for urban trans-portation funds, and is bored with the subject. It will not pro-duce a snappy lead. Readers will yawn at the tangle of fig-ures about bus routes, dollars, and population densities.

But the city will probably apply for transportation grants, and the topic might draw out differences between the incum-bent and his challenger, a thirty-six-year-old lawyer. Tom has made two calls to the challenger's campaign office and home, hoping for a reaction to the incumbent's release. But the can-didate is out shaking hands at plant gates and will spend the rest of the morning in house-to-house campaigning, putting him beyond media reach.

Tom debates what to do. The paper is loose today, and he has a crack at leading the local section. Typically he avoids stories about the grinding details of politics and government, the committee work, legislative action, issues. Tom has con-cluded that "readers are more interested in political intrigue and posturing and what candidates are like, their idiosyncra-sies and character."

He puts aside the transportation story and ponders a per-sonality piece about the incumbent. At a Rotary Club speech yesterday, he showed flashes of anger and frustration that the challenger was using age as an issue, pitting his jogging against the Congressman's jowls. "The cornered and prickly lion," Tom thinks. "Let's see if I can show his resentment and his pride in what he's done for the district." The outlines of a human-interest feature begin to take shape. He can include quotations from voters interviewed during visits to district neighborhoods, and from political old-timers at city hall. Re-calling the candidates' spirited exchanges at an unscheduled meeting last week will build excitement; he can contrast the two men's style and judgment.

Sentences stream onto Tom's computer display screen, and he feels a growing confidence that his profile will be given premium space at the editor's story conference later that morning, even if it does not lead the news section.

Later, Tom explains his reluctance to use issues in stories:

The straight issues are not good news because there's only one story in it, and it doesn't lead anywhere, or build any excitement. Even if the candidates disagree, it's a one-time story only. When it comes to choosing a Congressman, local voters seem much more inclined to base their decisions on such abstract qualities as personality, competence, and honesty, than on their positions. Perceptions are the facts. This is hard to do in a story, particularly a print medium. What I try to do is give a montage, a feeling about the candidates, across a number of issues. This is the way I want to communicate the stuff; it's not really conscious, but I try to communicate a sense of the person and the setting.

Tom demonstrates his philosophy the next day when he covers a debate before the local Bar Association. The challenger attacks the representative's insensitivity to veterans' needs and his votes to eliminate benefits for flight training, a measure that could affect an aviation school in the district. We ask if this topic had been (or would be) covered: "No, it's a thicket out there. I don't have the time to make all the necessary phone calls, and without research and quotations from both sides, you can't write the story."

Tom is twenty-seven years old. His father is a high school principal 160 miles across the state, his mother a homemaker. Tom started school at the local junior college, dropped out for a year, and returned to nearby Central State University to major in journalism. He took no history, two courses in political science, and as little as possible in other social studies. He has been at the *Times* for five years. During a summer internship he proved his energy and ability to write quickly. He has been covering politics for four years, in both the Second District and the neighboring Fourth District.

Tom is married, plays in a softball league, drinks a few scotches on weekends, and hopes to move on to a larger metropolitan paper someday. He makes $18,300 a year; his wife adds another $9,000 from her secretarial job in a local furniture manufacturing plant. They plan to have children if he can build a good file of clips, perhaps win some state journalism awards, and get into higher paying newspaper assignments.

Tom hopes to move away from politics. It's feast or famine, he says, and does not provide a steady menu of good story possibilities. He covets a copy editing position now open on the sports desk, finding the "routine and predictable working hours" attractive.

Tom's career and attitudes are familiar—his limited formal education, aversion to issues, eagerness to move into other assignments. The first day we spent with him demonstrated another lesson for challengers. They can miss a chance to crack the press with an issue stand by being unreachable during key, pre-deadline minutes.

The scene shifts to one of the country's largest metropolitan papers. Arline, twenty-six, is painfully aware that she graduated from college only four years ago, that she has been writing "Style Section" features, kitchen talk, and religious news ever since, and that she has just been asked to cover 19 congressional districts. In her first assignment she will arrange nine interviews with incumbent House members, over a two-day whirlwind trip to Washington, D.C. It is May 23; before June is over, 19 stories about district races will have run in the paper, and she will glow with the accomplishment.

Why was she handed the assignment? "I don't understand," she confesses. "I knew absolutely nothing about politics." She had to pick the brains of congressional staff members and politicos around the state, compiling source lists for each district. She wrote personalized stories, full of human-interest detail about the candidates' vulnerability to defeat and their campaign style. But information about their issue stands and political constituencies also made the paper. Stories longer than 20 column inches were common, and her copy received "sympathetic editing," not the slash and cut that often greets news of low priority.

"Assigning me to politics might seem like a sign of management's apathy," Arline says, "but no one could doubt the sincerity behind giving my material the dominant space and play it received." A look through her clipping file confirms this; the *Bulletin* often led sections with her stories, used artwork, and gave many remote districts a prominence that is hard to understand.

The *Bulletin* is aggressively trying to build statewide circulation, but this does not seem to explain its lavish allocation of time and space to the congressional races. Arline was told to hunt out the tightest and most interesting contests for follow-up coverage, and some of these were outside the paper's primary circulation zone.

Did she have trouble getting access to challengers? Not the "serious" ones, which means the candidates who were well financed and running a professional campaign. She dug into FEC reports and devoted several days to following candidates around their districts, looking for revealing tidbits of temperament and their "way with voters."

The oddest aspect of Arline's new beat, aside from the choice of reporter itself, was her relationship to the editorial endorsement process. One day in early October, by the elevator door, she bumped into an editorial writer retreating to his den on the floor above. She boldly asked who the paper had decided to endorse in the Eleventh District and got an evasive reply. Two days later she was called into a meeting with the editorial-page staff and asked for her impressions about the candidates she knew best. The staff had been letting the subject of congressional endorsements slide, but ended the campaign by endorsing in more races than usual, thanks to a slow elevator.

After the election, Arline was in a quandary about what to do next. She was asked to stay with state politics, but she felt burned out, exhausted by the daily campaign grind and uncertain whether the flow of political news is sufficient to keep an ambitious reporter fueled with bylines and good page placement. "There's bound to be a stretch of four to six months when there will be few stories to write," she realizes. The struggle to keep her contacts alive and her newsroom visibility intact discourage her from continuing with the beat.

Finally, we travel to a 55,000 circulation paper that penetrates two sprawling districts, one with a downtown business center showing ragged signs of prolonged depression in the automobile industry, the other marked by several prosperous agricultural towns.

Jack's election coverage is an example of what planning and resources will permit. He talks with us in the *Tribune's* fashionable conference room, tirelessly chewing gum; despite this habit, he is controlled, precise, even visionary about journalistic priorities.

"I do the backgrounders, and have the freedom of time to study FEC reports and pry into important stories affecting the campaigns." He stays in the office. Two other reporters, Chris and Steve, write the daily routine stories—pursuing releases, covering debates, attending the larger rallies and speeches.

"It hasn't always been this way at the *Tribune*," Jack explains. "Two years ago, Frank handled Congress. He was our political reporter, now reassigned to the editorial page, a title we don't use anymore. Frank used to do tracking stories, traveling around with the candidates for several days, writing a lot of personality stuff. This was his interest, his personal inclination. Now Chris and Steve rarely interview the candidates or do profiles. They do most of their work over the phone."

The three reporters this year have published less copy than one did before. Breaking news is handled by Chris and Steve in the field. Investigative material, which yields discouragingly few stories for each staff hour invested, is Jack's responsibility.

But this division of labor has been effective. The *Tribune* was able to break a story showing that an incumbent had diverted a Small Business Administration loan from a firm in which he had interests into his campaign treasury. "I worked 12 days to get a line on that one," Jack boasts. He also writes backgrounders about the congressional role, what members do with their time. He uses *Congressional Quarterly* as a reference, and his editor will even reprint articles from it if they have local relevance. Jack reads FEC reports closely and analyzes the political significance of contributions and campaign expenditure strategies. This digging finds its way into lean stories, not rambling personality sketches. Our rigid techniques of content analysis would not do justice to the way the *Tribune* covered the elections.

Jack is quick to judge the merits of different candidacies according to their professionalism in press relations. He scorns "playing games" with releases—leaking to one paper on its deadline and holding back from another. He bridles at an incumbent's contrived letter-writing campaign faulting one of his stories. Jack does not object to criticism, but disdains such clumsy ways of expressing it.

Candidates or aides who do not return telephone calls

earn a predictable contempt. The advantages of talented staff in the Washington office emerge as a profoundly important part of the incumbency edge. "When the candidate is traveling, staff is unreachable in the district. The Washington office can be relied on for facts, quotations, and other materials. They're professionals and know how the news business operates."

Three of the four candidates have been scheduling one or two press conferences each week. But for the life of him, Jack cannot understand why. "We have gotten away from covering that sort of thing." His paper, the dominant one in the two districts, has larger aims.

Jack is a product of a midwestern Catholic university. His journalism training there was practical, no frills. He is thirty-two, married with one child, respectful but not chummy with others, organized, liked by his editors.

After the election, the chain that owns Jack's paper decided to move him to the Washington bureau. Nothing could have pleased him more.

The experiences of Tom, Arline, and Jack draw together many of our discoveries about press attitudes and behavior. Each reporter is young. Each is struggling upward from middle-class origins. The newspaper world with its ready access to powerful and interesting people is an exciting departure from their parents' lives. These young journalists worked while in college, concentrated on practical studies, and emerged determined to succeed. They have careers to make, incomes to increase, families to establish. Regular bylines, visible assignments, a steady flow of recognition from superiors, will feed their ambitions. Agonies over relationships between press and government are alien to their thinking. If they can arrange it, the congressional election will be someone else's burden in two years.

Tom's and Arline's editors are like them, only older. Elections are not planned for; they are coped with. Staff meetings are not scheduled to identify each district's priorities or to plot reporters' time for maximum effect. It is assumed that evolving campaigns will set their own agenda for coverage, and that these will somehow mesh with each day's dummies, layouts of available space yielded by ad sales.

Electoral politics is the dog beat of newsrooms. Bright, energetic reporters do not linger long before they are off to more secure assignments, central to the newspaper's market position, such as business news, local government, or sports.

Our expert sources found Tom, Arline, and Jack—and the battalion of reporters for whom they stand—familiar. Our discussants were cheered by signs of innovation, but sensitive to the structural and managerial factors constraining the work of most reporters. Newspapers will not take electoral politics seriously, they reasoned, until they see readership gains to be won by nurturing competition in the political marketplace of ideas. Congressional races will languish in the shadows as long as journalists wait passively for others to create media events.

Many discussants recognized the problem of indifference toward challengers. But they offered a deeper excuse than the lassitude, inexperience, and political naïveté of reporters or the fondness of editors for the status quo. Here is their preferred explanation, distilled from several voices.

Political parties often concede districts where they cannot make a respectable showing; this is confirmed by our discovery that 22 of the 108 sampled districts in 1978 were uncontested. Some discussants speculate that concession in one area can generalize into a journalistic dubiousness about challenging incumbents elsewhere. In a self-fulfilling prophecy, expectations of failure translate into patterns of news and endorsement neglect that help solidify defeat.

The behavior of some candidates validates this view by the press. When challengers see their assault falter, they often "walk away" from the campaign, refusing to invest further in the effort. Media shrink from getting trapped in covering an abandoned contest; they can be expected to hold back from intensive coverage until assured that a race will be vigorously fought.

The weakening of parties aggravates the situation. Candidacies are increasingly mounted as individual, careerist stabs at office. Enduring party interests have withered. The press recognizes that unlucky challengers usually slink away to be replaced by other newcomers in two years. A lasting band of political activists—in short, a party—does not remain behind, picking up the pieces and continuing to assert the defeated challenger's programs. Without diehards in the bleachers, the press and candidates play to a shifting crowd, declining in numbers.

We take some exception to this plausible argument. It fails, for example, to explain why we find the greatest imbalance in news play in hotly competitive races, and in elections where papers have made endorsement choices. In an atmosphere of keen spectator interest, self-fulfilling processes should be weakened, not strengthened.

But this view by newspeople and political operatives builds a frame around their recommendations, to which we now turn. Our discussants, generous with their time and ideas, are practical people, inclined to find causes for individual journalistic behavior in a political system with overwhelming inertia. The ideas they offer for improving press performance express attempts to work within existing arrangements between newspapers and campaigns; they are not revolutionary prescriptions or calls for wholesale political change.

We view the simplicity of the suggestions that follow as a strength, not cause for derision. Each idea could be implemented easily. Each is offered by experienced journalists and political figures who are convinced that the quality of electoral reporting can be improved. We have sought to preserve our friends' air of modest but useful reform.

Suggestions for the Press

We were frequently reminded that the most fundamental force in all of politics is money. FEC reports are a bonanza, but one that can be bungled through quick interpretation or uninformed and unselective use.

"Early money is sleazy money," advised one informant. So "find out who is bankrolling candidacies at the early, crucial stages." Look for links between House members' PAC funding and their committee assignments and vote record. Search for "possible conflicts between PACs and local district interests."

This type of in-depth reporting requires a commitment many papers are unwilling to make. Reporters capable of this work earn higher salaries and may produce fewer-than-average column inches of usable copy.

*

Incumbents have mastered subtle arts of press relations. They visit publishers and senior editors, to be taken into the newsroom afterward and introduced to the (often new) reporter covering politics. No wonder if this reporter infers a friendship between two power brokers in the community, Representative X and Publisher Y.

Newspapers can counter these influences by self-conscious planning. An hour's meeting could provide reporters with leads on which issues and personality traits might be used in comparing the two contenders. Conflict is the stuff of competition. A reporter briefed about what to look for will be less blinded by the halo radiating from power elites.

Several discussants raged about their newspapers' general lack of campaign planning.* Few efforts are made to train new reporters (Tom and Arline are stunning examples). What preparation there is takes a mechanical form: deadlines for copy or arrangements to publish a tabloid section five days before the balloting. The reporter's knowledge about candidacies, as we have seen, is rarely tapped by the editorial-page staff.

Elementary, common-sense tactics of management could be borrowed from advertising or circulation departments. "We'd have a lot better news product," suggested one of our discussants, "if substance received as much care as delivery time." She may have exaggerated the point, but only out of exasperation.

*

Cute narrative leads, breathless quotations, and other slick journalistic styles are currently in favor. The *Washington Post* and the front page, left column, of the *Wall Street Journal* have taught fledgling reporters across the land: news can be bright and fun. Some have learned this lesson so well that

*Paletz and Entman (1981: 82) also note journalists' lack of preparation for covering issues.

the urge to write dramatically crowds the story aside. The clarification of an issue requires plain sentences that march solidly ahead. A candidate's psyche, temperament, or character invites more contrived expression.

If newspapers want to showcase issues, they had better think about presentation and display. One reporter suggests point-by-point comparisons between contenders. "Skip the daily story," he advises; "that's window dressing anyway." Assign periodic campaign stories that bring readers up to date on what has happened, where the candidates' support originates, and whose interests they will protect in office. "Information, not literature, is what the public needs," he says. Devious plots and psychologizing are the province of fiction, not journalism.

*

"The nature of elections invites sloppy, uncaring journalism," according to two veterans. The election result is news; the campaigning before is a grinding, grueling bore. Or, as one sighed, "I would rather have a tornado. It's over in a day, and you can get a prize for covering it."

There is a shiver of truth to this. Elections keep happening, with metronomic regularity. The city editor's most natural response: how did we do it last time? Let's keep overtime to a minimum. It is hard to preach against this wave of numbness without invoking homilies about the press in a democracy.

*

Beware of the incumbents' cloak of news exclusivity. For them, campaign rhetoric and congressional work are inseparable, and challengers are not permitted to get a word in edgewise.

The House is caught in a flurry of activity just before adjournment in mid-October, leading to a surge of news releases. This "news" fuels the representative's final weeks of campaigning.

Challengers are trapped by a journalistic reluctance to see "official" acts as electoral events. Tom's point of view illustrates: "Well, if the story is about Congress, say some bill the [incumbent] introduced or voted on, I feel no pressure to get the [challenger] involved."

Our discussants insist that journalists struggle against this asymmetrical philosophy of news judgment. It is the most vicious harvest from the store of incumbency advantages.

*

The indifference of readers to political stories is widely assumed by our discussants. But they offered ideas to combat this, born of their own accomplishments and those of news magazines and trailblazing papers like the *St. Petersburg Times*:

Clear page two or page three of advertisements (costly, but not unheard of). Start local election stories there, and jump to later pages only when absolutely necessary.

Keep stories short and to the point; run more of them.

Display stories attractively: use art work and typographic devices—at least to the extent that they are granted to food and style sections.

Index political and government news generally, herding it together for easier reader access.

Pay attention to how *Time*, *Newsweek*, and *U.S. News and World Report* get a political story across—with drawings, charts, boxes, and other tools. Clear writing with active verbs excites interest and aids comprehension too.

Predictable position in the paper is crucial. The lesson from CBS's show "60 Minutes" is inescapable. Its ratings remained stuck at a discouraging level as long as the network yanked it around in the schedule and rudely preempted it for other fare. Given a stable time slot (for newspapers, predictable page position), the program's fortunes blossomed.

*

Challengers need early coverage for name recognition and fund-raising credibility. Incumbents, of course, use their office as a constant platform for coverage. Where newspapers hoard staff and newshole, investing only late in campaigns, they play into the officeholders' hands.

Each newspaper must judge for itself when the campaign has begun, since a clap of thunder rarely heralds the start. Of course, any member of the House knows the campaign is under way month in and month out. The press can arbitrarily decide that a challenger's efforts deserve recognition at the filing deadline, or the day after the primary, or on Labor Day, or whenever. This decision shapes the public's opportunities to learn about candidates.

*

None of our discussants called for greater editorial support for challengers across the board. But they did not hesitate to describe the writing and argumentation in editorial columns as generally shallow, clumsy, and unhelpful to voters.

Contrast the contenders, they urged, as in the following hypothetical case:

> Smith is trying to unseat the two-term incumbent Jones in the Eighth Congressional District race, on a campaign pledge of greater fiscal responsibility. We find Smith long on rhetoric and short on specifics, and recommend returning Jones to Washington for another two years.
>
> Here is how the *Journal* compares the two candidates on water policy and urban development—key issues affecting the quality of life enjoyed by people in the Eighth District. . . . And so forth.

*

The frustrations among reporters at metropolitan papers are especially acute; they face a swarm of districts that bisect their circulation zones. A determined effort to cover all races often leads to single stories about each—a thin diet of information.

A more novel approach, illustrated by the paper at which one of our discussants worked, requires dedicated staffing and time for background research. The reporter was dispatched to find common elements that united several districts. In some instances these were needs arising from similar demographic features; elsewhere similarities were found in the candidates' campaign styles or in the districts' political histories. Stories were then topped with leads emphasizing these similarities as a consideration voters faced in making their choice "in the Seventh, Twelfth, and Thirteenth districts." Unfortunately, readership data are not available to test whether this approach increased the voters' interest or comprehension.

*

Staff turnover is high on the political beat. Managing editors might take stock of their newsrooms, noting where longevity and experience collect and where transience requires constant retraining. If newspapers prize experience in following campaigns for the superior coverage it yields, they will have to create incentives to keep reporters on the job. Bonuses in pay, stimulating assignments between elections, assurances that between-election preparatory work is valued by management, or a visible career path leading to more prestigious work can reward and stabilize reporting expertise where it is needed.

*

How can reporters make their world more bearable and professionally rewarding? Our discussants offered some answers:

Look on campaigns as an occasion to extend contacts that can be rewarding to your career. As one put it, "Politics, like sewers, goes everywhere and carries everything." Interest groups and power brokers swarm around candidates and will notice energetic and informed journalism. Though their immediate goals may be endangered by good reporting, their long-range purposes require contact with intelligent and trustworthy sources of information. Reporters can qualify to be recognized as such.

Spread your home phone number around. Campaigns are not confined to 8–5 developments. Accept the election as an opportunity, not a chore.

Recognize that good reporters give information as well as gather it. Know things that can be traded for things you do not know. Become recognized as someone who is valuable to talk with.

Avoid early judgments about candidates. Do not allow yourself to be sold on any of them, however charming or honorable, believing you should help some candidate win a deserved victory.

Think of yourself as a political journalist throughout the year, even when you store information rather than writing for tomorrow's edition.

Studies of the behavior of reporters have noted a continuum stretching from self-starting to "conveyor-belt" habits (Cohen 1963). At one end are reporters who seize chances to fashion the agenda of public attention; at the other end are reporters who prefer a stenographic role, responding to news as it is created by sources. A unifying theme in our discussants' suggestions is that journalists should take charge of the news agenda, especially when covering challengers; reporters must manufacture their own news priorities, rather than waiting for story leads to drop in their laps. This requires initiative, not passivity.

*

Incumbents usually outgun challengers on issues. House members sound more professional and assured, facts and figures at their aides' fingertips. Furthermore, incumbents can adopt an Olympian pose, making their contenders come across as adversarial and contentious.

Where reporters bring their own agenda to campaigns, they can force candidate interviews into new channels. Contenders may emerge as balanced in skill and style, though differing in viewpoint.* Where a challenger reveals an unsuspected awareness of ideas, greater journalistic investment is warranted.

*Not all candidates seek or even facilitate press access. Incumbents confronting a weak challenger may follow the adage offered by an informant of Matthews (1960: 207): "When you've got the votes, you don't have to talk."

In short, reporters can design their own test for electoral credibility and dig deeper into the merits and liabilities of the challengers who pass it.

*

Open races may occur unexpectedly, as when a seemingly popular incumbent is upset in the primary. Or they may be anticipated. Any newspaper should immediately recognize that open contests are a special opportunity to inform voters and to counterbalance the leverage exerted by large campaign contributions. The task of building public awareness should not be lightly abandoned to PACs and other special interests.

Reporters can be reassigned from more conventional political races—at local or other levels—and newshole could be reserved in amounts that would not be justified in those electoral frays. Attention to other elections or news might be sacrificed in order to capitalize on heated contests and heightened reader interest.

*

Our discussants shared a number of ideas for feistier editorials. Although entrenched incumbents facing a lackluster challenge are hardly the stuff of dramatic endorsement decision making, closer contests may warrant an in-house debate between the candidates. "Turn the newspaper's conference room into a competitive arena," we were advised. "Assemble a small gathering of reporters and editors to quiz the candidates."

Spirited give-and-take, provoked by questions from the floor, would not only produce good editorial copy; it would help educate younger reporters as well.

*

"Editors of the editorial pages can use the reporting staff as eyes and ears more effectively." Impressions gained by watching the interplay between a candidate and the public are worth sharing; in the process older editors can alert younger reporters to twists and turns in the local political process.

One editor put it bluntly: "There's no way a forty-three-year-old editor like me is going to accept endorsement advice from a twenty-three-year-old beginning reporter. I know she thinks the incumbent is an old fuddy-duddy. But I can learn things through her and tell her what sources to guard against in the district." More papers should arrange this interdepartmental contact, he felt.

*

Another editor pondered our findings on the modest levels of pre-endorsement effort (i.e., interviewing candidates or other sources) at some papers. "You know," he remarked, "when you've been around as an editor, you are familiar with political figures; as soon as they announce, you know where your stand will be."

We conceded as much, but asked why the reluctance to interview should be especially pronounced where the decision is a collective one (most commonly by an editorial board). He chuckled: "I think you and I agree there; no one wants to take responsibility, and to do the hard work that is required." This editorial-page editor made his paper's endorsement decisions himself, but hinted that he would prefer a strong, even intrusive publisher to committee action.

*

One paper we visited offered the following technique. It had endorsed a candidate, but had also published a chart showing the endorsements each candidate had received from other papers, both weeklies and neighboring dailies. "This shows people that the press can be subjective and fair at the same time."

*

One editor explained the press's fondness for endorsing incumbents this way: "You don't want to go for the newcomer just because he or she is younger, brighter, or more dynamic. Only the challenger who is *dramatically* better deserves support." Or, as he analogized, "Would you divorce your wife, just because you met a prettier woman?"

This adds up to a forbidding shield of logic, indeed, for challengers to pierce.

*

Editorials are more than stands for or against candidates; they are ways for papers to position *themselves* politically—to send signals to local elites about alignments the newspaper wishes to encourage and interests it seeks to block. This strategic meaning to editorializing could lead to endorsing candidates, not on their individual merits, but on the basis of their membership in a favored coalition. "Editorials are often elaborate semaphore flags," one discussant cautioned. "It's difficult for distant outsiders to decipher their hidden meaning."

*

Discussants reflected not only on our results, but also on those of Fenno (1975), Parker and Davidson (1979), and other political scientists who have noted the irony of a situation in which Congress as an institution is held in poor regard but individual representatives are esteemed. Parker and Davidson, in an attempt to explain this puzzle, analyzed the results from two national surveys. These data suggest that Congress as a whole is increasingly judged in a bad light because of its record on domestic policy, its adversarial relations with the Executive Branch, and the style and pace of the legislative process. Individual House members, on the other hand, are evaluated favorably because of their constituent services and personal characteristics.

Our data provide a glimpse into campaign coverage—a mere six weeks out of a representative's two-year term in office. But our discussants call attention to the press as a partner in reinforcing the public's schizophrenic view of Congress and its members.

If representatives' views were exposed to public evaluation and debate, their hold on power might be less forbidding. If challengers' stands on the issues provoked reporting about conflict, shifts from consensual to controversial politics might be fostered. Under the prevailing patterns of press coverage, however, we can expect continued dissatisfaction with the House but reluctance to blame its members for this malaise.

*

One political aide mused late in our visit: "Isn't there some way for newspeople to get together, reflect on lapses in their trade, and establish higher standards of work?" The question was sobering, if not new. Journalists have often sought ways to promote ethical and skilled performance. But the most recent evidence (Johnstone et al. 1976) tells us that fewer than half belong to a professional association. The scattering of newspeople across more than 1,700 daily papers and thousands of other workplaces has frustrated efforts to clump the bulk of them into a formal group. Here and there news councils have been formed; some papers appoint ombudsmen. Commissions periodically call for collegial mechanisms to judge meritorious work.

In all these undertakings, one stands out: the development of critical press reviews. The most esteemed, the *Columbia Journalism Review*, tackles problems in the journalistic craft where good intentions fail to be matched by able performance, where powerful economic and political forces have warped the quality of news. Other magazines of this genre include *MORE* (now defunct, but published during 1978), *Quill*, and the *Washington Journalism Review*.

Attention to these magazines indicates an interest in the craft's ethical side, at least marginally. And we find this interest echoed in the quality of campaign coverage reporters submit and get published.

We have seen how incumbents on the whole enjoy an enormous edge over challengers in news attention. But preferential treatment does not flow uniformly from the reporters' computer terminals; some journalists and their papers, especially when covering the hotly contested races, are more imbalanced than others. We draw a nugget of cheer from the survey data. Where reporters read professional journals, incumbents and challengers received nearly equal treatment. Where journalists do not read them, the incumbency advantage in news play was substantial.

The incentive to follow professional issues in such publications may be nurtured by senior editors, who in turn are really responsible for more equal treatment of candidates. Or the urge may arise from a reporter's personal intellectual needs—which are expressed in balanced coverage. Whichever, regular contact with discussions about news ethics seems to make a difference in press performance. More equal treatment results.

Back to the aide's question. At the least, getting newspeople together through the medium of print can help raise standards of work. There is at least this modicum of encouragement in our results.

Suggestions for Candidates

Both news and political people offered a bundle of advice for challengers. So many are helpless without a trained press aide (sometimes doubling as campaign manager) who understands news deadlines, answers calls from the press quickly, and knows what will make a news story. The value of talented press relations goes beyond the adviser's importance as a news source. Campaigns that can afford the best staff buy even more delicate skills.

We followed Tom to a candidates' debate. When the final applause had stilled, the incumbent's manager appeared, slapped Tom on the shoulder, and announced with enthusiasm, "We're 2 and 0," referring to his candidate's presumed second win in two public confrontations.

Tom did not "need" the manager's interpretation. Nevertheless, words were exchanged, information traded. Before parting, the manager astutely cautioned Tom about wasting his valuable time: "You know we're clean on the veterans' thing; he [the challenger] would be better off picking on some other issue."

The precise content of these remarks is not as important as the camaraderie established between two professional observers of the political scene. Money makes helpful aides possible. Many challengers cannot attract support, never build a viable organization, fail to employ staff who interact with important members of the journalistic community, and not surprisingly, do not win.

Almost all our discussants pointed to the lack of slick press relations and political strategy among challengers. The incumbent's Washington office feeds media with background and access to certified news sources in and out of Congress—all dished up with an authoritative aroma. WATS lines fanning out from the House Office Building may be the incumbents' most formidable weapon.

With incumbents, the journalist can simply process information. With challengers, the reporter must initiate coverage and needs a little help from the campaigner.

*

Discussants were free with tips to ease a candidate's entry into news columns. Ideas skimmed off the top include:

Become personally acquainted with reporters and with assignment editors. Establishing this presence opens lines of communication.

Keep track of stories published in each of the district's papers. Reporters hesitate to write up the same old speech, so feed them new material at luncheon talks. Always have a text of remarks available before the address; this simplifies note taking and promotes accuracy.

A 20-minute speech should focus on a single theme, not five or six. "Resist the Sears catalogue approach to campaign oratory," one person advised.

Know press deadlines. Schedule the candidate's time in advance, and alert the news media so they can plan coverage. Phone the newspaper's assignment editor or city editor to discuss next week's schedule, picking up clues about what the paper plans to cover. "If the candidate expects news attention, he or she will do something a little special," said one of our discussants.

Recognize and accept differences between what the candidate feels is important and what the journalist considers of news value. Do not be surprised when a seemingly minor topic in an interview or speech is bannered in the lead or made into headline material.

Find at least one vulnerability of the incumbent's and grind away at it, using variations on a theme.

Plan important events for daytime, especially morning, avoiding costly overtime hours. Try for joint appearances through third parties (e.g., citizen groups, the League of Women Voters, professional associations).

Route the candidate into newspaper offices for "casual" visits. These encounters develop contacts, help shape impressions, and stimulate interest in the campaign.

Make sure the candidate is known and well regarded by opinion leaders who rub shoulders with reporters. "You just pick up this stuff," explained one reporter. "The word gets out that so-and-so is good."

Make special arrangements for individual reporters to meet and talk with the candidate. Seat them together on a car ride to speeches. Bring them together at the motel bar after fund raisers. Respond quickly with interview possibilities whenever a reporter seeks contact.

Recognize that most reporters are out of touch with the issues. A simple briefing sheet covering highlights of the reclamation project, defense contract, or other policy area will win a gratitude that translates into increased coverage.

Candidates for the House must understand the district's special needs, or should fabricate concerns that set their candidacy apart from races for governor, senator, state legislator, or another office. Give the press excuses to write about you, and not about all the races for office this season. One of our reporters put it this way: "The election roundup story smothers each contest in a typographical hash. . . . Column inches, but oblivion."

Be alert to bright and snappy phrases that simplify the campaign. Do not wear them thin with use; distributed selectively, catchy sayings will help reporters craft readable news leads, encouraging greater focus on the candidate's case.

Never act peeved because of bad treatment in the press or try to retaliate. Never say, "Your reporting about me is unfair, so I'm not talking to you anymore."

Perhaps the most important piece of advice, one that is brought forth most clearly from our own data, bears on candidate recruitment. A contender lacking political experience is blemished in the press's eye: a dependable category of information for building stories is denied the reporter. Time in grade at lower rungs of the political ladder builds name recognition, cements contacts with the press, provides legitimacy.

A Concluding Note

Finally, we return to journalism's feeble swipe at covering political issues during campaigns. The most common explanation, or excuse, is that readers are not interested; they will not follow reporters into the dense underbrush of debate over public affairs.

We have presented some evidence to the contrary. We analyzed a voter survey showing that people express an agenda of problems they expect Congress to handle; and the most politically involved voters are especially eager to evaluate candidates on the basis of issues.

In one important way, it hardly matters whether we or the routine excuses are correct. Press inattention to issues, especially when raised by challengers, has deep roots and requires a difficult cure. The roots start with journalism's shift from partisan to objective reporting styles, fostered by the rise of national media and national markets for information and goods (Schudson 1978). The objective standard celebrates what has been said over what may matter. And what is said by authoritative sources outweighs pronouncements by figures without the credentials of office or power.

Reliance on official sources, which grants advantages to incumbents, discourages writers from looking for the relevance between a candidate's character and his or her stand on the issues. Reporters often overlook the humanistic dimension that ties public policy to health and well-being, personal income, property, or jobs.

Sudden increases in the conventional kind of coverage of issues would probably reap meager benefits in affording the public a better understanding of either incumbents or challengers. A novel form of journalism is needed, focusing on the circumstances that shape people's lives, and drawing relationships between those circumstances and the platforms offered by contenders for office.

Intelligent journalists can perform this function without sacrificing their independence, even their objectivity. It is a matter of asking candidates and their aides the right questions. And of rendering answers and evasions in language that relates to personal needs.

If journalism continues to confine itself to the past experience of candidates, the public will be encouraged to view policy choices through a rear-view mirror. Divisiveness and contending principles will wither. The influence of the press will slide in favor of Political Action Committees and other well-heeled interests.

To be sure, some of the features of media and politics that we document may be tied exclusively to elections for the House. But our findings do not paint the press in vibrant tones in any case, nourishing a competitive and stimulating political system. If Americans sense a tired or complaisant Congress, an unimaginative press may be partly responsible.

Appendixes

Activity Survey

Candidate-Specific Questions

Have you interviewed or talked personally with (Candidate A/B) during the *election* period, since the primary? How many times has this happened?

	Incum.	Chall.
Never interviewed candidate	18%	21%
One or two times	28	18
Three, four, five times	23	34
Six or more times	31	27

Have you talked with people or groups who are endorsing (Candidate A/B) or making contributions to his/her campaign? What groups?

	Incum.	Chall.
No	51%	45%
Talked with one group	25	30
Talked with two or more groups	24	25

Has (Candidate A/B) held any press conferences during the general election period? How many of these have you attended?

	Incum.	Chall.
None	79%	72%
Few/Most/Almost all	21	28

Has (Candidate A/B) spoken to meetings of groups or organizations? How many of these speeches or talks have you attended?

	Incum.	Chall.
None	34%	44%
Few	55	46
Most/Almost all	11	10

Does (Candidate A/B) have a campaign manager or person in charge? Have you interviewed or talked personally to him/her about the campaign? How many times has this happened?

	Incum.	Chall.
No manager/no interviews	51%	53%
One, two, three, four meetings	25	20
Five or more meetings	24	27

General Questions

Have you had occasion to use the public library or reference sources to find out things about the candidates or their campaigns? What sources have you used?

None	40%
One source	25
Two or more sources	35

Have you talked with any other reporters about either of the campaigns? Are these reporters from your paper or from someplace else?

Haven't talked with others	13%
Talked with reporters from my paper	24
Talked with reporters from my paper and from other papers	63

During this campaign period, have the campaigns issued news releases that you have received? Have you read the releases carefully, skimmed them, or mostly not read them?

Have not received/Not read	17%
Skimmed	20
Read carefully	63

Have you received texts of speeches, issue papers, or other documents from the campaigns? Have you read the materials carefully, skimmed them, or mostly not read them?

Have not received/Not read	44%
Skimmed	21
Read carefully	35

Have you been reading wire service coverage of the (named) District campaigns?

No	59%
Yes	41

Have you been reading coverage of the (named) District by any other newspapers?

No	28%
Yes	72

Have you done anything, other than what we've talked about, to cover the campaigns or candidates during the general election period? What have you done?

Nothing	45%
Mentioned one activity	31
Mentioned two or more activities	24

Newspaper Sample

Abilene Reporter News (Tex.)
Altoona Mirror (Pa.)
Ann Arbor News (Mich.)
Appleton-Neenah-Menasha Post-
  Crescent (Wis.)
Atlanta Journal (Ga.)
Aurora Beacon-News (Ill.)
Austin American-Statesman (Tex.)
Bakersfield Californian (Calif.)
Baltimore News-American (Md.)
Bergen County Record (N.J.)
Binghamton Press (N.Y.)
Bloomington-Normal Pantagraph
  (Ill.)
Bridgeport Post (Conn.)
Burlington County Times (N.J.)
Casper Star-Tribune (Wyo.)
Charleston Mail (W. Va.)
Chicago Tribune (Ill.)
Cleveland Plain Dealer (Ohio)
Columbia State (S. Car.)
Columbus Republic (Ind.)
Dayton News (Ohio)
Denver Post (Colo.)
Detroit News (Mich.)
Elgin Courier-News (Ill.)
Elizabeth Journal (N.J.)
Elkhart Truth (Ind.)
Erie Times (Penn.)
Eugene Register-Guard (Ore.)
Flint Journal (Mich.)
Gainesville Times (Ga.)

Grand Island Independent (Neb.)
Grand Junction Sentinel (Colo.)
Greenville Reflector (N. Car.)
Hastings Tribune (Neb.)
Hazelton Standard-Speaker (Pa.)
Houston Chronicle (Tex.)
Indianapolis Star (Ind.)
Jeffersonville News (Ind.)
Jersey City Journal (N.J.)
Kansas City Times (Mo.)
Kingston Freeman (N.Y.)
Kinston Free Press (N. Car.)
Kirksville Express and News (Mo.)
Lexington Dispatch (N. Car.)
Lincoln Courier (Ill.)
Long Island Newsday (N.Y.)
Los Angeles Times (Calif.)
Louisville Courier-Journal (Ky.)
Lufkin News (Tex.)
Mansfield News Journal (Ohio)
Memphis Commercial Appeal
  (Tenn.)
Miami Herald (Fla.)
Middletown Times Herald-Record
  (N.Y.)
Milwaukee Journal (Wis.)
Minneapolis Star (Minn.)
Monroe News (Mich.)
Montgomery Advertiser (Ala.)
Mount Vernon News (Ohio)
New London Day (Conn.)
Newark Star-Ledger (N.J.)

Nyack Rockland County Journal
  News (N.Y.)
Oakland Tribune (Calif.)
Olympia Daily Olympian (Wash.)
Orange County Register (Calif.)
Orlando Sentinel Star (Fla.)
Philadelphia Bulletin (Pa.)
Pittsburgh Press (Pa.)
Pomona Progress Bulletin (Calif.)
Portland Press Herald (Maine)
Poughkeepsie Journal (N.Y.)
Redding Record Searchlight (Calif.)
Riverton Ranger (Wyo.)
Royal Oak Tribune (Mich.)
Sacramento Bee (Calif.)
Saginaw News (Mich.)
St. Louis Post-Dispatch (Mo.)
Salt Lake City Tribune (Utah)
San Angelo Standard (Tex.)
San Antonio Express (Tex.)
San Diego Union (Calif.)

San Francisco Chronicle (Calif.)
San Jose Mercury (Calif.)
Seattle Times (Wash.)
Sheboygan Press (Wis.)
South Bend Tribune (Ind.)
Sterling Journal-Advocate (Colo.)
Sunbury Daily Item (Pa.)
Syracuse Herald-Journal (N.Y.)
Toledo Blade (Ohio)
Toms River-Bricktown Observer
  (N.J.)
Topeka Capital (Kans.)
Tulsa World (Okla.)
Union City Dispatch (N.J.)
Washington Post (D.C.)
Waterloo Courier (Iowa)
Watertown Times (N.Y.)
Willoughby News-Herald (Ohio)
Wilmington Journal (Del.)
Winston-Salem Journal (N. Car.)
Worcester Gazette (Mass.)

References

References

Abramowitz, A. 1975. "Name Familiarity, Reputation, and the Incumbency Effect in a Congressional Election," *Western Political Quarterly*, 27: 668–84.

———. 1980. "A Comparison of Voting for U.S. Senator and Representative in 1978," *American Political Science Review*, 74: 633–40.

Andrews, F., J. Morgan, J. Sonquist, and L. Klem. 1975. *Multiple Classification Analysis*. Ann Arbor, Mich.

Arrendell, C. 1972. "Predicting the Completeness of Newspaper Election Coverage," *Journalism Quarterly*, 49: 290–95.

Arseneau, R., and R. Wolfinger. 1973. "Voting Behavior in Congressional Elections." Paper presented to the American Political Science Association, New Orleans.

Asher, H., and H. Weisberg. 1978. "Voting Change in Congress: Some Dynamic Perspectives on an Evolutionary Process," *American Journal of Political Science*, 22: 391–425.

Atwood, L. E. 1980. "From Press Release to Voting Reason: Tracing the Agenda in a Congressional Campaign." Paper presented to the International Communication Association, Acapulco, Mexico.

Bagdikian, B. 1974. "Congress and the Media: Partners in Propaganda," *Columbia Journalism Review*, Jan.–Feb.: 3–10.

Bernstein, C., and B. Woodward. 1974. *All the President's Men.* New York, N.Y.

Blumler, J., and M. Gurevitch. 1981. "Politicians and the Press: An Essay on Role Relationships," in D. Nimmo and K. Sanders, eds., *Handbook of Political Communication*. Beverly Hills, Calif.

Breed, W. 1955. "Social Control in the Newsroom." Reprinted in W. Schramm, ed., *Mass Communications*. Urbana, Ill., 1972.

Burnham, D. 1980. "Congress's Computer Subsidy," *New York Times Magazine*, Nov. 2: 96–101.

Burnham, W. B. 1975. "Insulation and Responsiveness in Congressional Elections," *Political Science Quarterly*, 90: 411–35.

Campbell, A. 1966. "Surge and Decline: A Study of Electoral Change," in A. Campbell, P. Converse, W. Miller, and D. Stokes, eds., *Elections and the Political Order.* New York, N.Y.

Cannon, L. 1977. *Reporting: An Inside View.* Sacramento, Calif.

Cantor, M. G. 1971. *The Hollywood TV Producer: His Work and His Audience.* New York, N.Y.

———. 1980. *Prime-Time Television: Content and Control.* Beverly Hills, Calif.

Chaffee, S. 1977. "Mass Media Effects: New Research Perspectives," in D. Lerner and L. Nelson, eds., *Communication Research—A Half Century Appraisal.* Honolulu.

Clapp, C. 1963. *The Congressman: His Work as He Sees It.* Washington, D.C.

Clarke, P., and S. H. Evans. 1980. "All in a Day's Work: Reporters Covering Congressional Campaigns," *Journal of Communication,* 30: 112–21.

Clarke, P., and E. Fredin. 1978. "Newspapers, Television and Political Reasoning," *Public Opinion Quarterly,* 42: 143–60.

Clarke, P., and F. G. Kline. 1974. "Media Effects Reconsidered: Some New Strategies for Communication Research," *Communication Research,* 1: 224–40.

Cohen, B. 1963. *The Press and Foreign Policy.* Princeton, N.J.

Comstock, G. 1980. *TV in America.* Beverly Hills, Calif.

Congressional Quarterly Weekly Report. 1977. Oct. 29: 2299–2311.

———. 1979. Sept. 29: 2151–63.

———. 1980. April 5: 889–936.

Cover, A. 1977. "One Good Term Deserves Another: The Advantage of Incumbency in Congressional Elections," *American Journal of Political Science,* 21: 523–42.

Cover, A., and B. Brumberg. 1982. "Baby Books and Ballots: The Impact of Congressional Mail on Constituent Opinion," *American Political Science Review,* 76: 347–59.

Cover, A., and D. Mayhew. 1977. "Congressional Dynamics and the Decline of Competitive Congressional Elections," in L. Dodd and B. Oppenheimer, eds., *Congress Reconsidered.* New York, N.Y.

Crouse, T. 1973. *The Boys on the Bus.* New York, N.Y.

Davidson, R., and G. Parker. 1972. "Positive Support for Political Institutions: The Case of Congress," *Western Political Quarterly,* 25: 600–612.

Dunn, D. 1969. *Public Officials and the Press.* Reading, Mass.

Epstein, E. J. 1973. *News from Nowhere: Television and the News.* New York, N.Y.

Erbring, L., E. Goldenberg, and A. Miller. 1980. "Front-Page News and Real-World Cues: A New Look at Agenda-Setting by the Media," *American Journal of Political Science,* 24: 16–49.

Erikson, R. 1976. "The Influence of Newspaper Endorsements in

Presidential Elections: The Case of 1964," *American Journal of Political Science*, 20: 207–33.

———. 1978. "Is There Such a Thing as a Safe Seat?," *Polity*, 4: 623–32.

Fenno, R. 1975. "If, as Ralph Nader Says, Congress Is 'The Broken Branch,' How Come We Love Our Congressmen So Much?," in N. Ornstein, ed., *Congress in Change: Evolution and Reform*. New York, N.Y.

———. 1978. *Home Style: House Members in Their Districts*. Boston.

Ferejohn, J. 1977. "On the Decline in Competition in Congressional Elections," *American Political Science Review*, 71: 166–76.

Fiellin, A. 1967. "Recruitment and Legislative Role Conceptions: A Conceptual Scheme and a Case Study," *Western Political Quarterly*, 20: 271–87.

Fiorina, M. 1977a. *Congress: Keystone of the Washington Establishment*. New Haven, Conn.

———. 1977b. "The Case of the Vanishing Marginals: The Bureaucracy Did It," *American Political Science Review*, 71: 177–81.

Fishel, J. 1973. *Party and Opposition: Congressional Challengers in American Politics*. New York, N.Y.

Fiske, S. T., and D. R. Kinder. 1979. "Schematic Understanding of Political Leaders." Paper presented to the American Psychological Association, New York, N.Y.

Fowler, L. 1979. "The Electoral Lottery: Decisions to Run for Congress," *Public Choice*, 34: 399–418.

Gans, H. 1979. *Deciding What's News*. New York, N.Y.

Gieber, W. 1964. "News Is What Newspapermen Make It," in L. Dexter and D. M. White, eds., *People, Society and Mass Communication*. New York, N.Y.

Glantz, S., A. Abramowitz, and M. Burkart. 1976. "Election Outcomes: Whose Money Matters?," *Journal of Politics*, 38: 1031–38.

Goldenberg, E., and M. Traugott. 1979. "Resource Allocation and Broadcast Expenditures in Congressional Campaigns." Paper presented to the American Political Science Association, Washington, D.C.

Graber, D. 1971. "The Press as Opinion Resource During the 1968 Presidential Campaign," *Public Opinion Quarterly*, 35: 168–82.

———. 1980. *Mass Media and American Politics*. Washington, D.C.

Greenberg, B., and P. Tannenbaum. 1962. "Communicator Performance Under Cognitive Stress," *Journalism Quarterly*, 39: 169–78.

Halberstam, D. 1979. *The Powers That Be*. New York, N.Y.

Hecht, B., and C. MacArthur. 1928. *The Front Page*. Reprinted in B. Cerf and V. H. Cartmell, eds., *Sixteen Famous American Plays*. New York, N.Y., 1941.

Hess, S. 1981a. *The Washington Reporters.* Washington, D.C.

———. 1981b. "Fear and Fraternity in the Washington Press Corps," *Washington Journalism Review,* Jan.–Feb.: 37–41.

Hinckley, B. 1980a. "House Re-elections and Senate Defeats: The Role of the Challenger," *British Journal of Political Science,* 10: 441–60.

———. 1980b. "The American Voter in Congressional Elections," *American Political Science Review,* 74: 641–50.

Hohenberg, J. 1960. *The Professional Journalist.* New York, N.Y.

Huckshorn, R., and S. Spencer. 1971. *The Politics of Defeat.* Amherst, Mass.

Hynds, E., and C. Martin. 1977. "Editorial Writers Tell How They Go About Their Work," *Journalism Quarterly,* 54: 776–79.

———. 1979. "How Non-Daily Editors Describe Status and Function of Editorial Pages," *Journalism Quarterly,* 56: 318–23.

Inter-university Consortium for Political and Social Research (ICPSR). 1979. *The American National Election Study, 1978.* Ann Arbor, Mich.

Jacobson, G. 1975. "The Impact of Broadcast Campaigning on Electoral Outcomes," *Journal of Politics,* 37: 769–93.

———. 1978. "The Effects of Campaign Spending in Congressional Elections," *American Political Science Review,* 72: 469–91.

———. 1980a. *Money in Congressional Elections.* New Haven, Conn.

———. 1980b. "Candidates, Campaigns, and Contexts in Congressional Elections." Paper presented to the American Political Science Association, Washington, D.C.

———. 1981. "Strategic Politicians and Congressional Elections." Paper presented to the American Political Science Association, New York, N.Y.

Jacobson, G., and S. Kernell. 1981. *Strategy and Choice in Congressional Elections.* New Haven, Conn.

Johnstone, J., E. Slawski, and W. Bowman. 1976. *The News People.* Urbana, Ill.

Kaid, L. 1976. "Newspaper Treatment of a Candidate's News Releases," *Journalism Quarterly,* 53: 135–37.

Katz, D., and R. Kahn. 1966. *The Social Psychology of Organizations.* New York, N.Y.

Kelley, D. 1959. "Press Coverage of Two Michigan Congressional Elections." *Journalism Quarterly,* 35: 447–49.

Kinder, D. 1976. "Leaders and Their Images: Misperceiving Presidential Candidates, 1968 and 1972." Paper presented to the Midwest Political Science Association, Chicago.

———. 1978. "Political Person Perception: The Asymmetrical Influence of Sentiment and Choice on Perceptions of Presidential Candidates," *Journal of Personality and Social Psychology,* 36: 859–71.

Kinder, D. R., R. P. Abelson, S. T. Fiske, and M. D. Peters. 1979. "Impressions of Political Leaders." Paper presented to the American Psychological Association, New York, N.Y.

Kingdon, J. 1966. *Candidates for Office: Beliefs and Strategies*. New York, N.Y.

Klapper, J. 1960. *The Effects of Mass Communication*. New York, N.Y.

Lang, K., and G. E. Lang. 1953. "The Unique Perspective of Television and Its Effects: A Pilot Study," *American Sociological Review*, 18: 3–12.

Lasswell, H. 1948. "The Structure and Function of Communication in Society," in L. Bryson, ed., *The Communication of Ideas*. New York, N.Y.

Lazarsfeld, P., B. Berelson, and H. Gaudet. 1948. *The People's Choice*. New York, N.Y.

Leuthold, D. 1968. *Electioneering in a Democracy: Campaigns for Congress*. New York, N.Y.

Lippmann, W. 1922. *Public Opinion*. New York, N.Y.

MacKuen, M., and S. Coombs. 1981. *More Than News: Media Power in Public Affairs*. Beverly Hills, Calif.

Mann, T. 1978. *Unsafe at Any Margin: Interpreting Congressional Elections*. Washington, D.C.

Mann, T., and R. Wolfinger. 1980. "Candidates and Parties in Congressional Elections," *American Political Science Review*, 74: 617–32.

Markham, J. 1961. "Press Treatment in the 1958 State Elections in Pennsylvania," *Western Political Quarterly*, 14: 912–24.

Mason, W. 1973. "The Impact of Endorsements on Voting," *Sociological Methods and Research*, 1: 463–95.

Matthews, D. 1960. *U.S. Senators and Their World*. Chapel Hill, N.C.

Mayhew, D. 1974. "Congressional Elections: The Case of the Vanishing Marginals," *Polity*, 6: 295–317.

———. 1976. *The Electoral Connection*. New Haven, Conn.

McClenghan, J. 1973. "Effects of Endorsements in Texas Local Elections," *Journalism Quarterly*, 50: 363–66.

McCombs, M. 1976. "Editorial Endorsement: A Study of Influence," *Journalism Quarterly*, 54: 545–48.

McGinnis, J. 1969. *The Selling of the President, 1968*. New York, N.Y.

McLeod, J., and B. Reeves. 1980. "On the Nature of Mass Media Effects," in S. Withey and R. Abeles, eds., *Television and Social Behavior: Beyond Violence and Children*. Hillsdale, N.J.

Miller, S. H. 1978. "Reporters and Congressmen: Living in Symbiosis," *Journalism Monographs* No. 53.

Mintz, M., and J. S. Cohen. 1976. *Power Inc.: Public and Private Rulers and How to Make Them Accountable*. New York, N.Y.

Nie, N., S. Verba, and J. Petrocik. 1976. *The Changing American Voter*. Cambridge, Mass.

Nimmo, D. 1964. *Newsgathering in Washington*. New York, N.Y.

Noelle-Neumann, E. 1973. "Return to the Concept of Powerful Mass Media." Reprinted in E. Dennis, A. Ismach, and D. Gillmor, eds., *Enduring Issues in Mass Communication*. St. Paul, Minn., 1978.

O'Keefe, G., and L. E. Atwood. 1981. "Communication and Election Campaigns," in D. Nimmo and K. Sanders, eds., *Handbook of Political Communication*. Beverly Hills, Calif.

Olson, D. 1978. "U.S. Congressmen and Their Diverse Congressional District Parties," *Legislative Studies Quarterly*, 3: 239–64.

Ornstein, N., T. Mann, M. Malbin, and J. Bibby. 1982. *Vital Statistics on Congress, 1982*. Washington, D.C.

Paletz, D., and R. Entman. 1981. *Media Power Politics*. New York, N.Y.

Paletz, D., P. Reichert, and B. McIntyre. 1971. "How the Media Support Local Government Authority," *Public Opinion Quarterly*, 35: 80–92.

Parker, G., and R. Davidson. 1979. "Why Do Americans Love Their Congressmen So Much More Than Their Congress?," *Legislative Studies Quarterly*, 4: 53–61.

Peterson, T. 1956. "The Social Responsibility Theory of the Press," in F. Siebert, T. Peterson, and W. Schramm, eds., *Four Theories of the Press*. Urbana, Ill.

Polk, L., J. Eddy, and A. Andre. 1975. "Use of Congressional Publicity in Wisconsin District," *Journalism Quarterly*, 52: 543–46.

Polsby, N. 1980. "The News Media as an Alternative to Party in the Presidential Selection Process," in R. Goldwin, ed., *Political Parties in the Eighties*. Washington, D.C.

Pool, I., and I. Shulman. 1959. "Newsmen's Fantasies, Audiences, and Newswriting," *Public Opinion Quarterly*, 23: 145–58.

Ranney, A. 1979. "The Political Parties: Reform and Decline," in A. King, ed., *The New American Political System*. Washington, D.C.

Rivers, W. 1965. *The Opinionmakers*. Boston, Mass.

Robinson, J. 1974. "The Press as King-Maker," *Journalism Quarterly*, 51: 589–94.

Robinson, M. 1981. "Three Faces of Congressional Media," in T. Mann and N. Ornstein, eds., *The New Congress*. Washington, D.C.

Roshco, B. 1975. *Newsmaking*. Chicago.

Rosten, L. 1937. *The Washington Correspondents*. New York, N.Y.

Russonello, J., and F. Wolf. 1979. "Newspaper Coverage of the 1976 and 1968 Presidential Campaigns," *Journalism Quarterly*, 56: 360–64, 432.

Sanoff, A. 1975. "Double Reverse at the Free Press," *Columbia Journalism Review*, 13: 47–51.

Scarrow, H., and S. Borman. 1979. "The Effects of Newspaper Endorsements on Election Outcomes: A Case Study," *Public Opinion Quarterly*, 43: 388–93.

Schudson, M. 1978. *Discovering the News*. New York, N.Y.

Shaw, D. 1977. *Journalism Today: A Changing Press for a Changing America*. New York, N.Y.

Sigal, L. 1973. *Reporters and Officials: The Organization and Politics of Newsmaking*. Lexington, Mass.

Snowiss, L. 1966. "Congressional Recruitment and Representation," *American Political Science Review*, 60: 627–39.

Songer, D. 1981. "Voter Knowledge of Congressional Issue Positions: A Reassessment," *Social Science Quarterly*, 62: 424–31.

Stempel, G., III. 1973. "Effects of Performance of a Cross-Media Monopoly," *Journalism Monographs* No. 29.

Stokes, D., and W. Miller. 1966. "Party Government and the Saliency of Congress," in A. Campbell, P. Converse, W. Miller, and D. Stokes, eds., *Elections and the Political Order*. New York, N.Y.

Superman: From The Thirties to the Seventies. 1971. New York, N.Y.

Swanberg, W. A. 1961. *Citizen Hearst*. New York, N.Y.

Talese, G. 1969. *The Kingdom and the Power*. New York, N.Y.

Tedin, K. L., and R. W. Murray. 1979. "Public Awareness of Congressional Representatives: Recall Versus Recognition," *American Politics Quarterly*, 7: 509–17.

Thompson, H. T. 1973. *Fear and Loathing on the Campaign Trail '72*. San Francisco.

Thrift, R., Jr. 1977. "How Chain Ownership Affects Editorial Vigor of Newspapers," *Journalism Quarterly*, 54: 327–31.

Tuchman, G. 1972. "Objectivity as Strategic Ritual: An Examination of Newsmen's Notions of Objectivity," *American Journal of Sociology*, 77: 660–79.

Tufte, E. 1973. "The Relationship Between Seats and Votes in Two-Party Systems," *American Political Science Review*, 67: 540–54.

Tunstall, J. 1971. *Journalists at Work*. Beverly Hills, Calif.

Vermeer, J. 1978. "Candidate Press Releases in the 1973 New Jersey Gubernatorial Campaign." Paper presented to the Midwest Political Science Association, Chicago.

Wanat, J. 1974. "Political Broadcast Advertising and Primary Election Voting," *Journal of Broadcasting*, 18: 413–22.

Waugh, E. 1937. *Scoop*. Boston.

Wright, G. 1978. "Candidates' Policy Positions and Voting in U.S. Congressional Elections," *Legislative Studies Quarterly*, 3: 445–64.

Zajonc, R. 1980. "Feeling and Thinking: Preferences Need No Inferences," *American Psychologist*, 35: 151–75.

Index

Index